Empowered by Hope

Ha T. Tran

authorHOUSE®

AuthorHouse™
1663 Liberty Drive
Bloomington, IN 47403
www.authorhouse.com
Phone: 1-800-839-8640

© 2010 Ha T. Tran. All rights reserved.

No part of this book may be reproduced, stored in a retrieval system, or transmitted by any means without the written permission of the author.

First published by AuthorHouse 4/30/2010

ISBN: 978-1-4490-6931-5 (e)
ISBN: 978-1-4490-6929-2 (sc)
ISBN: 978-1-4490-6930-8 (hc)

Library of Congress Control Number: 2010902507

Printed in the United States of America
Bloomington, Indiana

This book is printed on acid-free paper.

Read What Others Are Saying About *Empowered by Hope:*

"This book is a must read! When I read the story of how this great family overcame the challenges of the falling of Saigon, and how Ha herself went from a life of opulent comfort, to being sent off to the United States, then rose again to be successful in spite of her circumstances, I got goose bumps. Her Dad, Mr. Nguyen Van Tho, is an incredibly wise man, a strong man who has had many victories in life, but he will be proud to receive his autographed copy of his beautiful daughter's book covering her life's work and knowing how she is helping other people live a better life and overcome their limitations—keeping her Dad's wisdom alive."

STEVEN L. KEOUGH, a.k.a. "Coach Steve", author of ***Straight Forward Coaching*** and ***Self-Esteem***

"This book is a genuine source of energy! It serves me as a 'portable spare battery' for my soul. The wisdom and life experience Ha shares is truly uplifting and pure inspiration. The strongest part is that everything Ha says comes from her own life experience. She actually LIVES the inspired story she is telling. Thank you Ha!"

TOMAS TILVER, professional writer and translator, Sundbyberg, Sweden

"I first encountered Ha when she was a guest on my wife's radio show. I listened to her story, not so much as a curious Vietnam vet, but more as a curious human being with empathy for a woman who shared struggles similar to my own…despite the vast cultural divide between us. When I heard her speak in person for the first time at a meeting of In the Presence of Positive Women, I knew that I wasn't the only Vietnam vet in the room. I could sense the beginning of a wonderful friendship…a kinship if you will (Ha now refers to me as her brother). The story of her struggles and her victories over them cannot help but inspire. Her love affair with a man she met once before they were married warmed my heart and will warm yours. Having served as a combat medic for a year in her country may have made our friendship more likely than had I served as an infantry-man…

the truth is, I can't imagine any bigger obstacle than what my 'sister' Ha and I share."

RICK ADAIR, founder, this Field, Center for Beginner's Mind

"Empowered by Hope is one of those rare books that touches the hearts of the masses. Its universal message of hope is sincere and inspiring for all ages. This poignant true story is simply captivating."

DEB DUNHAM, author of *Tween You and Me: A Preteen Guide to Becoming Your Best Self*

"Ha's story will inspire, awe, and chill you with her seemingly unending trials. She and her husband, Quang, remain striking examples of what the human mind and spirit can overcome. I invite you to make the discoveries that I have experienced."

KENNETH C. CRANNELL, Ph. D., Crannell Consulting; author of *Voice and Articulation*; Professor Emeritus, Emerson College

"Empowered by Hope is a touching story and an amazing journey of a woman who has learned to find her voice through *all* those loving little life lessons she learned through her father's teaching and is now applying here for all who come into her path."

SHERRI RAFTERY, DTM, 2009-2010 Governor Toastmasters District 31

"Based on lessons learned from childhood, Ha Tran delivers a timeless book of inspiration and hope that transcends barriers of creed, race, and culture. The thread weaving itself throughout Ha's book is the gift of love and wisdom from her father. Through the uncertain journey from Vietnam to an unknown country filled with new struggles, the gift from father to daughter appeared as his voice in her mind, empowering her day by day. Ha used her priceless gift to become a successful businesswoman and respected inspirational speaker. Now, she shares the wisdom found in her father's gift, lessons learned in her childhood, and the visions and philosophy that empower. This inspiring book has a place on everyone's desk, night stand, or table to provide a daily message of wisdom to live in the present with the vision of hope."

PAUL KEENE, Keene Health LLC

"We are often faced with the difficult choice of either taking a risk in life or submitting and becoming resigned to 'this is just the way things are.' Ha Tran took this risk and literally gambled with her life. Ha's message and experience of taking a big risk in order to create a better life for herself is powerful stuff indeed. If you have a passion to live a full and significant life, you will want to read this book."

JONATHAN MANSKE, Cerebral Sanitation Engineer, author of *The Law of Attraction Made Simple*

"Your father as your ideal; your inspiration; and your Asian respect to parents is most moving. Younger generations sometimes take things for granted. Your work should be spread and read by young students, to understand fear, sacrifice, love, and the desire to improve our daily lives and break the 'poverty cycle.' What I read brought tears to my eyes, since often we forget how many people are constantly toiling and suffering to live, or many times merely survive. Your father taught you strong and good moral principles to abide and follow. You, and your father, make us remember what the price is to reach the 'American Dream.' Many blessings to your father, and your family."

RAY SERRA, retiree, US Armed Services; professional photographer

"Life is an experience we share through our stories. How we tell these stories can bring a smile, teach a lesson, and sometimes, even in our darkest hours, bring *hope*. Travel along as a young woman embarks on a journey that will take her to a new life full of challenges and opportunities in a new land. With her she carries a precious gift, the words and wisdom shared by her father. He could not join her on the journey, so instead he gave her the best part of himself, his wisdom and his hope. And now, as she shares her story, she passes on this precious gift to you so that you too can be empowered by hope."

JOAN KOERBER-WALKER, Chairman, CorePurpose, Inc.; Chairman, The Opportunity Through Entrepreneurship Foundation

"***Empowered by Hope***—indeed! We can all learn valuable lessons from Ha's journey. She embodies true hope and has risen like a phoenix to exemplify what is great about this country. Only in America could a 'boat person' rise from nothing to a position of helping others navigate the waters of their lives. Yet, it is about so much more than just a land of opportunity...

Inspired by the unbelievable love that her father demonstrated (how many of us would sacrifice a future with our children so selflessly?!) she has taken the wisdom passed on to her and used it to help others. Yes, hope is indeed alive and well!"

A. DRAYTON BOYLSTON, founder, Rescue Institute; author of ***Coming Unscrooged! A Contemporary Classic of Corporate Rescue and Redemption***

"'Keep living your life until you draw your last breath,' words of wisdom given from a father to his daughter that penetrated the depths of her soul. Words that led Ms. Tran on an expedition of discovery that took her across the globe from a country embroiled in war to a land that promised a life of freedom. ***Empowered by Hope*** is a true story of survival, vision, hope, love and possibility where none previously existed. Ha Tran exemplifies what it means to take even the deadliest obstacles and turn them into amazing experiences that will inspire you while taking you on your own journey of awe and respect for one so humble and yet so brave; a woman who shares the story of many others who never had the chance to tell it to the world. When you read ***Empowered by Hope*** you will be changed forever."

KATHLEEN GAGE, author of ***The Law of Achievement***

"Reading ***Empowered by Hope*** is a gift you can give yourself. You can read Ha Tran's story of her life after she escaped from Vietnam after the war. As a story it's a wonderful read. More than that, though, reading it can be a transformative experience, because Ha Tran uses her story to convey her father's unique philosophy of life, truly Empowered by Hope. With so much trouble in our world today, this gift is perfectly timed. Enjoy!"

RICK BRENNER, author of ***Go for It! Sometimes It's Easier If You Run***

"Ha Tran's beautiful, powerful book, ***Empowered by Hope,*** is moving and insightful. She freely and humbly shares her experiences and wisdom gained from her father's love, her arranged marriage and her perilous journey out of Vietnam. Her story is courageous. Her work is one of simple truth and her genuine love for our planet shines through. This is a great read!"

DR. DENISE LAMOTHE, professional speaker, Clinical Psychologist, Doctor of Holistic Health, Emotional Eating Expert, author of ***The Taming of the Chew: A Holistic Guide to Stopping Compulsive Eating***

"This book is real, genuine, and heart-felt. The great story of Ha's journey and the important life lessons her dad passed on to her is educational, inspiring, up-lifting, and highly motivational. If you want to be filled with hope and belief that you can achieve great things regardless of your situation or the odds you face, I highly recommend *Empowered by Hope*."

JOHN J. CHAPIN, author of *Sales Encyclopedia*

"*Empowered by Hope*, Ha's captivating story of her life in Vietnam, escape from an oppressive regime, and her struggle and triumph in her new country is an inspiration for us all. This book is beautifully written, with her father's inspiring philosophy woven throughout. It will definitely captivate you!"

TOM ANTION, author of *The Ultimate Guide to Electronic Marketing for Small Business*

"Ha is an extraordinary human being who had a book inside her dying to get out. This is her true, inspirational story about her unrelenting passion and her dangerous escape to freedom. A planned marriage and her father's wisdom sustained and protected her throughout her journey of hope. She empowers us to examine our own lives and helps us to fight for the freedom in our hearts."

DAVE COHEN, DTM, founder, Well Spoken

Viet Nam

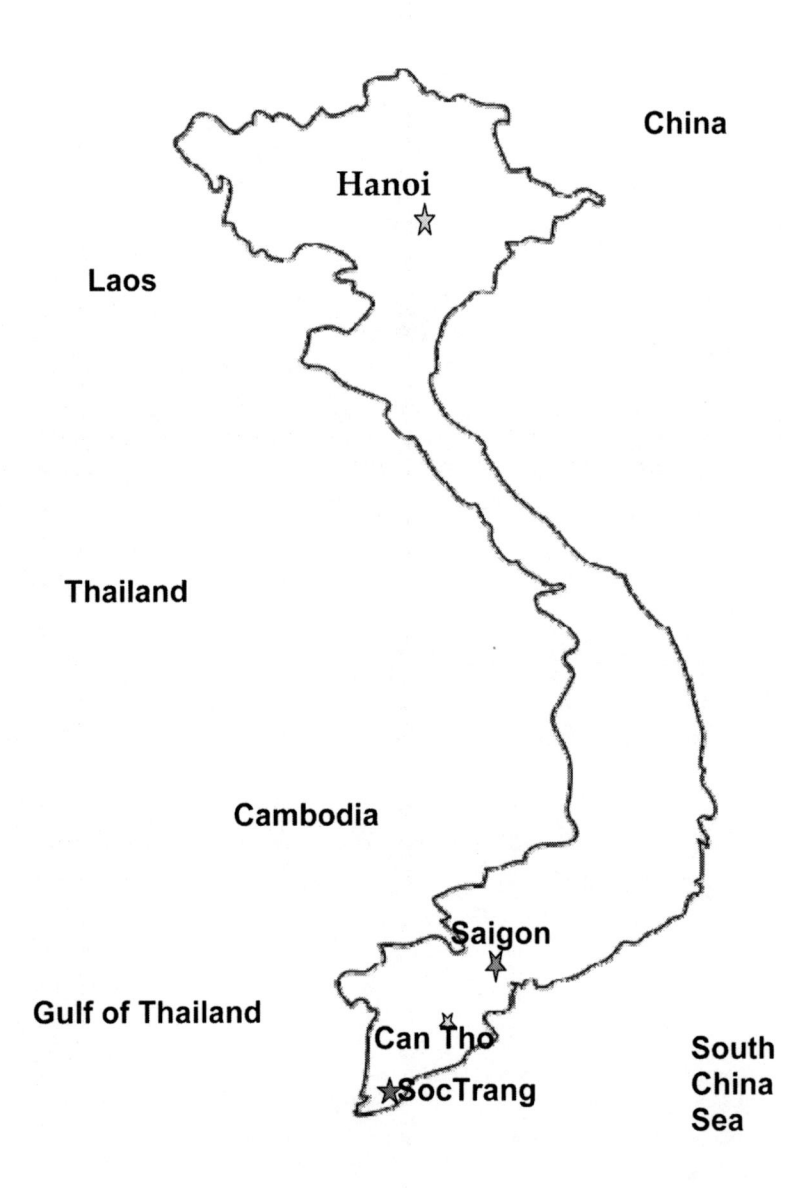

China
Hanoi
Laos
Thailand
Cambodia
Saigon
Gulf of Thailand
Can Tho
SocTrang
South China Sea

Acknowledgements

My father is still alive and living in Vietnam at the age of 99. I owe him a profound debt of gratitude for loving me enough to make huge sacrifices.

I thank him for the gift of my life. For the lessons that have sustained me and helped me conquer obstacles. For granting me the chance to discover that one moment in time when I would find the true meaning of living life with a promise in my heart. Without his deep and endless love and support I would not be here.

Thank you to my friends who have nurtured and supported me to this point in my life and who have contributed to ***Empowered by Hope***. Having you in my life is a heart-felt privilege.

The individuals who have made this book possible are counted among my very best friends and great supporters who believed in me and listened to my endless stories: Carmen J. Scarpa, John and Linda Knight, Nancy Ignazi, Mary Bell, Emilie Missud, Linda O'Connor, David Cohen, Dr. Kenneth Crannell, Tracy Keller, Iris Weaver, Rick and Debby Adair, Tony and JoAnne Corrao, and Jackie Rose. I owe you all a great debt of gratitude. Thank you for providing me with a safe and nurturing environment, for allowing me to make mistakes and for loving me despite my shortcomings.

To Nancy, Tracy, and Iris, my everlasting thanks for the transcribing, typing, editing, and unending support. Thank you to Mary Bell for my father's photograph and to Carolyn Sheltraw for a lovely book cover design.

For all of my teachers and mentors who believed in me before I believed in myself: Carmen J. Scarpa, Dr. John Knight, Dr. Kenneth Crannell, Charlie Gindele, Noreen Reilly, A. Drayton Boyston, Steve Keough, Kathleen Gage, and Tom Antion. You rock!

To my friends and sponsors in Illinois: Beverly and Fred Flachentrager, Helen and Jack O' Halloran, Mary Jane and Dr. Applington, Catherine and Dr. Doyle, Loretta and Dr. Leydon, Helen Haskin, Lorena and James Robinson, Jane and Dr. Duncan, Sally and Jim Wright, Carol and Jim Stevenson, and Sally Krats—I'm deeply indebted to all of you.

To my children: Matt, Ikumi, Calvin, Eileen, Kristina, and Rebecca; my grandchildren: Ella, Davis, Caden, and Spencer—I love you and thank you for being who you are, my precious gifts.

To my husband, Quang, for your patience, love, and support, and for allowing me to be as mysterious, wild, and crazy as I can be when I'm "chasing clouds."

With love and gratitude, you all have my best always and all ways.

Carpe diem!

Ha

Dedication

I want to express my profound gratitude to my father, for he is love personified. My journey has been a long, tough and often rough road. Dad, you are the brightest star shining in the galaxy, taking me upward as I follow you. You are my compass in life! Your wisdom enlightens and inspires me. I have found that your thoughts and dreams inspire and enrich all the people's lives you touch. I am honored to be your daughter.

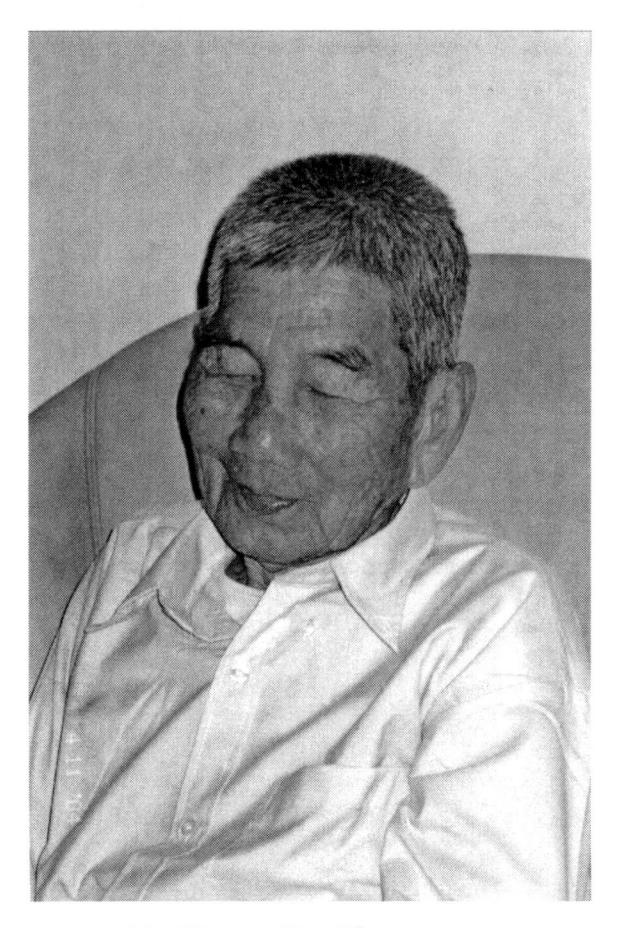

Mr. Nguyen Van Tho at age 88

Author's Note

This book is about the lessons I learned in my childhood from my father. He instilled his philosophy and values in me. I was his avid pupil.

Like any parent, my father hopes that I have continued with the lessons he taught me. I have always tried to live by his words. Because we live so far apart, he has not witnessed what powerful tools those words have been for me, how they've impacted my life. It was my great fortune to inherit them.

My father's philosophy is not new or revolutionary. However, it is powerful because of where it came from—far away and long ago, full of love and good intentions.

The ideas expressed in this book are based purely on my memories of and interpretation of my father's words and philosophy. The proof of how effective they are is my own experience.

Table of Contents

Acknowledgements	xi
Dedication	xiii
Author's Note	xiv
Introduction	1
Chapter One: Lessons Learned	3
Chapter Two: Hold On…	10
Chapter Three: …And Never Give Up	13
Chapter Four: Stay in the Present	17
Chapter Five: Be Disciplined and Fight the Good Fight	22
Chapter Six: Do Your Best, Be Honest…	26
Chapter Seven: …and Keep Your Promises	29
Chapter Eight: Let Your Vision Guide You, But Your Passion Lead You	32
A Ha Moment: Essays	37
Letters from the Heart	59
Words Of Wisdom From Sam Antion	67

Quotes from Mr. Nguyen Van Tho

"No matter what, you must live your life until you take your last breath."

"A promise is a promise to keep and to deliver."

"Live life with no regrets: let your vision guide you and your passion lead the way."

"Do your best, be honest, and keep your promises."

"If you don't hit the finish line, you forfeit the chance to be a winner."

"Say what you mean, mean what you say, just don't say it mean."

"When you're a parent, you parent someone from the moment they're born till the moment you die."

Introduction

Imagine...

Marriage to a stranger...a journey to freedom full of uncertainty, danger, and desperation...life in a refugee camp...arriving in a country that before now had been just a name on the map.

In this country, no one looked like me: All the people I met on the street resembled the faces of the men and women in uniform I had seen only on the news fighting in my country's war. Everything was strange.

In April of 1975 Vietnam fell to the Communists. We lived in South Vietnam, and the new regime was brutal to the residents of this part of the country. My father had to make a difficult decision: He decided I should escape the country.

He didn't want me traveling alone, so he arranged for me to marry my husband, a stranger ten years older than me.

It was two-and-a-half years before we could finally leave the country, and almost another year before we arrived in the United States.

My two young sons, my husband, and I arrived in Chicago with twenty dollars and one suitcase.

We learned enough English to communicate our everyday needs, but adjusting to this new country and culture was very hard with a language

I still have trouble getting my tongue around. I worked very hard, but it took so much courage and determination to keep making the effort day after day.

I was determined to enjoy my freedom, pursue a good quality of life for our family, and honor both my old and new cultures. My husband's main concern was providing the daily necessities for our family. He was beaten down by the tremendous effort it took to do that in this unfamiliar land.

I was the one who wanted to make sure that my children had all the opportunities I could see out there, who wanted to take our family further. However, working so hard, many times I felt that I had no more energy to keep going.

My father's words were a gift I had not realized were with me. When I became so discouraged I felt I could not continue on, I suddenly heard his voice in my head: "Keep living your life until you draw your last breath." It was as if he had encoded his voice onto a computer chip and embedded it in my brain's memory bank.

All the times during my childhood that he had repeated his philosophy over and over had a miraculous power to keep me going. When I was at a low point, I remembered what he said and found his love gave me the strength to continue.

I missed my father so much in my first years in this country and wanted him still to be able to care for me. Although he wasn't here with me, he had given me the gift of his philosophy. Even though I still miss him to this day, his gift continues to carry me.

His sayings became the foundation I used to propel myself forward and achieve my dreams. They are priceless gifts I appreciate and will treasure for the rest of my life. I have used these gifts to guide and teach my children.

In putting his philosophy into practice I discovered what his words meant and how they apply to my life in the present.

By sharing my father's philosophy, I honor him and what he sacrificed for me, and I ensure that his wisdom lives on in those who carry it forward. I believe this is a timeless, universal philosophy of use to everyone.

It is my desire, my joy, and my great honor to share what I have learned with you and it is my sincere hope that it will help you live your life to the fullest.

Chapter One: Lessons Learned

Of all the things my father taught me, there were two things above all he wanted me to remember. As I was leaving Vietnam, he kept saying: "Do your best, be honest, and keep your promises" and "No matter what, you must live your life until you take your last breath." These two pieces of wisdom have carried me my whole life.

My father knew what I would need to survive, and that he had to give me the words that would act as a life preserver in a stormy sea. These became words for *survival*.

Mr. Nguyen Van Tho, my father, is a wonderfully wise man. He lived his life and let me watch, teaching me by example. When he did say something, he would back it up with his actions. For example, he always told me to be truthful and I witnessed him being truthful with others. He didn't just preach ideas to me, he lived them. He truly "walked the walk."

It was a powerful way to teach his precious daughter, his only child. Being impressionable as any young child, his words and actions became deeply embedded in my being.

Because my mother had died when I was eight years old, he felt that he had to make up for her absence and give me everything that both a mom and a dad would.

We had an intellectual tradition in my home while I was growing up. I remember spending time with my father in our library, which was a large room with floor to ceiling bookcases, filled with books on philosophy and literature. I was expected to do well in school and after graduating high school, I entered law school.

My dad was also fond of inspirational quotes that illustrated his principles and our home was dotted with fabric banners, framed quotes, and plaques bearing these sayings. To this day I have a love of quotations and inspirational sayings.

I had a privileged life growing up in Vietnam. My father was a wealthy rice merchant and we lived in a big house on a big plot of land which was beautifully landscaped. I wore beautifully tailored clothes made of silk and always had plenty of delectable food to eat.

I even had my own little companion, a girl my age named Mai, who waited on me at my beck and call. She called me "Little Miss" and her job was to play with me and pick up after me. Mai lived in our house from the time we were both very young. My father had made a financial arrangement with her parents, which I started to understand when I was about 12 years old. She even came to live in my apartment in the city of Soc Trang where I stayed during my last year of high school.

Then, on April 30, 1975, Saigon fell, the Americans left South Vietnam, the civil war was over, and the Communists took over the part of Vietnam where I was living. The atmosphere was paranoid because anyone could be arrested and tortured at any time. Fear and terror were the order of the day.

The fact that my father and I were educated and well off put us in further danger since education and personal wealth were seen as examples of capitalism. My father's property was confiscated, and that's when he knew we were going to be in real trouble.

In order to ensure my safety and survival he knew I must escape the Communist regime. I had to leave Vietnam, the only home I knew. I was twenty years old, and my father did not want me, his only child, to escape Vietnam alone.

Despite worrying for my safety if I traveled alone, his unconditional love brought him to the heartbreaking decision that he could not come with me. He thought that if we went together and were caught, he wouldn't be able to save either me or himself. So he stayed behind to ensure that if anything happened to me he could take the necessary measures to free me.

Still, he did not want me taking an uncertain journey into an unknown world by myself. He could have sent a servant with me but he believed a family member would be more loyal than a hired companion. He thought a husband would take care of me in his place and ensure my safety.

My father talked furtively with people he did business with, including my future father-in-law. He couldn't let anyone know what he was doing. If word got to the authorities, they would suspect we were trying to escape and we would be arrested.

One day my father came home and told me he had arranged for me to get married. That is how, seventeen days later, on October 27, 1975, I came to marry a stranger, someone I had met only once for half an hour seventeen days before.

There was no monetary dowry, one which would have been typical for a wedding in Vietnam. Instead my husband gave an emotional dowry, the promise to my father, and me, that he would care for, love, and protect me, my father's only child. My father's unconditional love gave him the strength to let me go, even though his world revolved around me.

My relationship with my husband was that of an acquaintance. We had to get to know each other over time. There had been no courtship or falling in love: This marriage of convenience meant I had to learn to get along with someone I had no choice but to be with.

After my family and I had escaped Viet Nam and survived in a refugee camp we came to the United States. Our first home on American soil was in La Salle, Illinois. Thanks to the largesse of ten women in a Bible study group, we arrived there in the winter of 1979. These ten wonderful sponsors guided and assisted us in our new life with great kindness, but it was extremely difficult for my family and me nonetheless. We did not speak any English, and the huge sense of cultural bewilderment was exacerbated by the language barrier.

In a few short years I had gone from a life of opulent comfort to living a dismal life of uncertainty. Life had to take on a new meaning for me.

It was during this time that I started to fully appreciate my father's words of wisdom and, eventually, integrate them into every fiber of my being and make them my own.

In order to survive and thrive, I had to understand what his ideas meant for me and how to implement them in my everyday life. Doing so has given me purpose, a road map for my life, and a never-ending determination to live my life to the fullest.

The journey of learning to live my father's wisdom has been entwined with my journey from Vietnam to the United States of America, from a pampered child to an adventurous, self-reliant adult.

Our eldest son Do with his grandfather in 1999

Our youngest son Dinh with his grandfather in 1999

Mr. Tho meeting his grandson Dinh's fiancé Eileen for the first time; this is the kind of vehicle I rode in when Dinh was born

Our two sons Do and Dinh, with their younger sister Tuyen

Our eldest daughter, Diem Nghi

Chapter Two: Hold On...

When the time did come to flee, my husband and I escaped Vietnam on a fishing boat.

We had been waiting for the right time and the right connections for two and a half years. During that time we bought passage on the boat.

****

We had no notice for leaving. Our guide simply showed up at the door of our hut and, without saying a word, signaled to us to pick up our children and follow him. In the middle of the night we snuck away. Quang, my husband, and I carried only what we could put on our backs and hold in our hands. Our most precious possessions were, of course, our sons: our one-and-one-half-year-old son, Do, and our 28-day-old infant son, Dinh.

We walked through rice patties with rough-cut stubble that painfully thrust into my feet and legs.

My right ankle was already broken. I had been thrown from a sidecar on the way to the hospital the day my youngest son was born less than a month earlier.

Chapter Two: Hold On...

There had been no one to reset it. A midwife delivered my son, but there was nothing that could be done for my ankle, because all the doctors had been put in concentration camps.

After the long, very painful struggle through the rice patties, we finally reached the river. A man with a small bark-canoe was waiting to transport us to the boat.

When I saw the boat, I was terrified. It was an old fishing boat that had been outfitted to hold far more than the maximum of 80 or 100 people it was meant to hold. The greedy owners stuffed over 400 people on board. None of us cared at the time, since this was our only way to freedom.

As soon as we got aboard, my husband and I were separated. He and our older son had to stand on the deck because there was no place for them to sit. I sat in the bottom of the boat near the engine hole, my baby in my arms. I was back to back, side to side with three other women. Breathing in nauseating diesel fumes, I felt suffocated and exhausted by the heat and the bodies pressing in on me. I was in excruciating pain, my bruised legs and broken ankle paralyzed beneath me.

When the boat started moving, I became extremely seasick. I couldn't eat or drink, nothing would stay down. I was totally drained.

I was breast-feeding Dinh, who was only 28 days old. Due to the lack of nourishment, my milk supply dried up, and all I could do for him was let him nurse for comfort. It was agony to hear my son crying his heart out for food and realize I had nothing to give him. He cried until he was so exhausted he could cry no more tears.

Because my mother had died when I was still a child, I hadn't had anyone to teach me about nursing and taking care of my babies. I thought my body would just keep producing milk endlessly no matter what.

I did not understand that I needed to ensure that I was properly nourished to be able to feed my son. When I had nursed Do at home I had had adequate food and drink. It never occurred to me that I might not be able to produce milk, so I hadn't thought about what to do if that happened.

After a day and a half at sea the old fishing boat's faulty engine failed. The captain said that all we could do was pray. So we prayed while the boat drifted.

I prayed hard to the spirit of my deceased mother, to Buddha, to God, "Please do not let us die on this journey."

We drifted for another day and a half. I lost consciousness from dehydration and heat exhaustion. I was carried up to the deck of the boat to get fresh air. Later, my husband told me that when he saw me, he was frantic. He thought I had died, and those people were just about to throw my corpse overboard. He didn't know where our baby was. He was thinking to himself, "How can I write home to tell her father that the boys and I have finally gotten to the refugee camp; however, she did not make it? She died during the exhausting ordeal!"

I woke up enough to feel rain water on my face, and then drifted into a dark but peaceful place of unconsciousness. I thought I had died and was going to enter Heaven. I started to prepare my case to Heaven. I pleaded, "I am not Heaven-worthy because I have failed my sons. I promised to them that I would be there for them from the first day of their existence and will always be there, but now I can't…So please send me back for me to make it right." There was only silence; I didn't receive a response. I turned to my baby in my arms, "Please forgive me, I have broken my promise to you and your brother…forgive me…" I said good-bye to my son.

****

I felt a soft touch on my shoulder. I opened my eyes to see a woman kneeling beside me. She was draped in white and helping me sit up. She wrapped a blanket around my shoulders and spoke to me in a soft voice, in a language that I did not understand. I thought she must be an angel.

She waved over another woman, also dressed in white, to bring me my baby. He was wrapped in a soft, blue blanket. He was finally peaceful, sound asleep and satisfied with a tummy full of formula.

Then the first woman pointed to the shore where my husband and son were standing. It wasn't until then I finally realized that I was alive.

Holding my baby in my arms, life was precious and being alive was wonderful!

I realized that I was on a rescue boat, and those women were nuns. The boat had picked us up and brought us to an island in Malaysia where we were given refuge.

Chapter Three:
...And Never Give Up

When we arrived in Malaysia, the port was crowded with people waiting to see if the boat held their family members or friends. Some of the waiting crowd found familiar faces on the boat, others asked for news about their relatives and were disappointed. No one was waiting for us.

In the refugee camp I was very sick. I had not yet recovered from pregnancy and childbirth when we left Vietnam. On top of that, I had broken my ankle the day my son was born, and it hadn't been properly set.

I was further depleted from nursing my son and not having been able to take in any nourishment on the boat. And from the time I had stepped onto the boat until several days in the camp I had not been able to go to the bathroom at all. My system was septic from all the built-up toxins. I was in really rough shape.

It was more than a week before I started to recover.

While I was struggling to get better, I was strongly aware that I needed to stay alive so I could take care of my family. My mind was constantly working, but my body was shutting down. There was nothing I could do so I prayed and prayed. I didn't know what would happen next; I could only wait for things to take their course. All I had were prayer and determination; my determination was bone-deep from the very core of my being. It gave me strength.

I remembered my promise to my father to never give up. He had sacrificed so much for me in his effort to give me a better life of freedom and a chance for happiness. My gratitude for his unconditional love and respect for his wishes made it impossible not to keep fighting with every ounce of my strength.

The way my father loved me taught me how to love my sons. I wanted and needed to be there for them, as he had been there for me.

My father had told me, "When you're a parent, you parent someone from the moment they're born until the moment you die." Because of my devotion to my family, I found the strength to keep going.

****

Our living quarters in the camp consisted only of a tent with a single long bed. We shared the bed with our sons and three other couples and their children.

The bed had been made from the wood of ship wrecks that drifted to shore. Each family was separated only by a cloth rice sack hung from the tent ridge pole and had only about four to five feet of space.

We received food and medicine from the American Red Cross and other relief agencies. We had mostly canned food plus fresh eels every other day.

Every morning my husband and three of the men who shared our tent waited in line for our rations. The other women in the tent cooked and visited with people they knew. They were polite to me but didn't try to make friends with me.

I wasn't able to do much at first because it was very difficult for me to move around. My broken ankle had not been properly set and I was in constant pain. The island was hilly and the ground was uneven which also hampered my movements.

After a few months, I started to make an effort to move around more. Unable to lift my foot, I dragged my right leg behind me with my baby clutched in my arms and my one-and–a-half-year-old son holding onto my pant leg.

We would go down to the sea shore. While I watched my sons play in the sand, I searched for the meaning of all this and wondered, "What next?"

Chapter Three: ...And Never Give Up

During this time, I felt so miserable that I questioned my faith in my father's decision, wondering if he had done the right thing.

Yet every morning I watched the sun rise. Every day was a new day with new hope and new possibilities. Every day was a reaffirmation of my promise to my father to "Live life until I took my last breath."

On the island, in the refugee camp, we waited a very long time for our interview. While we were waiting and waiting time stood still. Every day seemed much longer than twenty-four hours.

Each day I thought, "Maybe today will be the day we get picked for an interview." We didn't know what the system for choosing families was, or if there even was a system, or if it was just pure luck.

We did know, however, that once we'd been interviewed, we'd have a sponsor. We'd be able to settle in the United States or another first-world country where we'd be free and able to realize the opportunities we had only imagined. We were hoping for the U.S.

Then one day, after six long months of waiting, we were notified. We got scheduled for an interview. We were excited about it but there was no sponsor yet, only more waiting. And waiting....

What helped us get through the waiting was our ability to just keep going. We held onto hope and the possibility of a promising future.

And we learned to be patient. Sometimes what you need or want is not yet available and all you can do is wait.

A few months passed while our prospective sponsors were determined. At last they were found, and the paperwork had been cleared.

But then, after our sponsors had been confirmed, there was *still* a four-month waiting period in another refugee facility in Kuala-Lumpur, the capital of Malaysia. We were tested for infectious diseases and given immunizations. Meanwhile our sponsors were looking for housing for us, and preparing to meet the needs of an immigrant family.

We finally got our health clearance. *America, here we come!*

****

In November of 1979, we flew to O'Hare International Airport in Chicago from Kuala-Lumpur. After the plane had landed, we joined the exiting parade of people. We had our young sons between us and one small suitcase holding all of our clothes which had been donated by various relief organizations. We knew not a word of English and had a grand total of twenty dollars.

Everyone on the flight had someone waiting with open arms, except us.

We felt alone in that crowded airport. We moved slowly and awkwardly, clinging together. The fear of separation bonded us with invisible glue.

The airport was full of people going in every direction. Their eyes made no contact with ours. They were all in a hurry and nobody saw us. We were paralyzed with fear and anxiety.

We kept looking for our sponsors. We had been told that they would greet us at the airport. But we saw no one who seemed to be looking for us!

It was the most helpless, frightening feeling not to be able to ask for assistance or inquire if anyone was waiting for us.

Then, *finally*, we spotted the two women in the crowd. They were holding a sign that said *Quang Hon Tran*— my husband's name! At that moment, they were the most beautiful women in the world. I felt enormous relief. I was released from the paralyzing fear and I ran to them crying like I have never cried before. I wept like a lost child miraculously reunited with her parents.

Chapter Four: Stay in the Present

When my husband and I arrived in the United States, we couldn't spend time looking back at the past. It was too painful then, and we had a family to support.

We were in a large community but we were very isolated mentally and culturally. Having only our sponsors to communicate with, we were totally dependent on them to take care of us, and teach us how to function in our new culture. We relied on them for many things such as taking us shopping, setting up appointments, and going to the doctor.

My husband and I learned to stay in the present while we were working to establish our new life. We didn't know the power of staying in the now until we were forced to do so by circumstances.

If we concentrated on what we were doing today, we would do a much better job than if we were worrying and wondering about what we'd be doing tomorrow. It wasn't until much later that we realized what a valuable lesson we had learned.

Although we learned not to fret about what we would be doing tomorrow, we always had tomorrow in mind. It was like laying bricks—you put down one brick, and then another brick, and then another.

Looking at each brick individually, it seems like not much is happening. However, when they are all put together, you soon find that you have built a wall to protect yourself. What we did today was the foundation for what we would do tomorrow. We felt that we were building steps for our children to stand upon.

Our struggle was similar to the growth of the bamboo plant. Since I have been living in America I often hear people talk about the bamboo plant and how it is a metaphor for the mystery and mastery of promising results.

In the Vietnamese culture, bamboo is a symbol of strength, flexibility, tenacity, endurance, and promise. When it is first planted, it doesn't seem to be doing anything for the first few years. The real action is going on under the ground during the first two to three years. It grows roots, penetrating deep into the soil, becoming grounded.

Then it puts out more roots, spreading in its new location. It is not until the third year that the bamboo starts putting out shoots above ground. The stalks come thrusting up from the nodes which occur every few inches or foot or so, every future leaf compactly folded in place, ready and willing to come out.

My family's future was built one brick, one node, one compact future leaf at a time.

****

First I had to master our new country's tongue. Mrs. Flaschentrager and Mrs. Duncan, two of our sponsors, were my first tutors. Their lessons were simple. They'd come to my apartment with a bag of items and pull out a pencil, a key, a can. They'd say, "Pencil." I'd repeat it. Then, "This is a pencil." And I'd repeat that. We worked our way to, "How are you?" "I'm fine, thank you. And you?"

The cultural and language barriers became abundantly clear when our sponsors attempted to discuss family planning with me. They figured we had two children already and they knew that in the U.S. large families were an economic liability. Their first concern was to make sure our family didn't grow any larger.

Our sponsors were ten kind, beautiful, well-to-do, proper Midwestern women, who all belonged to the same Bible study group. Unfortunately, they didn't speak any Vietnamese or Chinese.

Chapter Four: Stay in the Present

Imagine ten very proper ladies trying to explain the concepts of sex and birth control to Vietnamese boat people. Family planning and related matters were never discussed between strangers or even immediate family in Vietnam.

They're not to blame for the fact that I now have four children! Imagine how you'd go about bringing up sex and family planning to strangers, especially when they didn't speak one word of your language.

First my friends tried sign language. I found their gesticulations odd and very strange. I didn't sign, and the motions they were made were very confusing.

Then they tried drawing pictures. I wasn't sure what they were trying to tell me. I thought they might be alluding to sex, but surely they would not talk about *that* with me!...or would they? I was amazed that they would try to have this conversation at all.

I'd thought we'd just share tea and sweet dumplings. Not these pictures and these drawings!

I sat patiently as they tried to make a connection with me. They were frustrated. I, on the other hand, was frightened because they were upset and I couldn't understand why. Now I can laugh about it.

In the course of learning about sex, birth control, and family planning, we had two more children!

****

When we were newcomers to this country, my husband and I couldn't understand what people were saying in English. We would look at their faces trying to get a clue as to what they were saying. However, the meaning of most facial expressions differs from culture to culture. What is meant by a particular expression in my culture may be very different in your culture.

Trying to communicate simply by looking at facial expressions becomes a very tricky proposition. The only two expressions that are universal are sadness and happiness. Everything else is up for grabs.

In Vietnam people do not express their feelings on their faces. We are taught to keep everything inside and only let our feelings show through our eyes. This is why we watch each other so intently during conversations.

Because we don't generally communicate through facial expressions, we are at a tremendous disadvantage when we arrive in a place where people do show their feelings on their faces.

My husband and I would try to discern what was meant by looking at our sponsors' faces. If someone was laughing or smiling, we would say "yes." If we looked at a face and our interpretation of it was serious, we would say "no." It had nothing to do with what was actually being said to us.

To further confound communication with our sponsors, however, we would very respectfully say "yes" before we said "no." The Vietnamese way of respectfully accepting or declining is "yes, yes" or "yes, no." But by saying "yes" and then "no," we only sounded confused or unsure since our sponsors didn't know about our culture's rules of etiquette.

Eventually our sponsors figured out that we'd answer yes or no even when we didn't understand what was being said. They would make sure that we understood them, rather than just letting us automatically answer.

****

My proficiency in English did not come easily.

I wanted to be able to communicate my thoughts, my concerns, and my feelings. How was I to go from expressing my thoughts in Vietnamese to expressing them in English?

My first English lessons had been with our sponsors. I also learned English, including how to form simple sentences, by watching television, *Sesame Street* and *Mr. Rogers* with Mr. Feeney the mailman. My children, of course, had no problems with the language in school or with their friends.

I would read children's books aloud to my children, in part to help my English. I enjoyed fairytales and other simple kids' books, but Dr. Seuss was a challenge with all his tongue-twisting words.

I had to overcome difficulty with pronunciation, especially words with *l*, *r*, *rl*, and combinations of those sounds. It was an effort I made every day, focusing my time and energy so I could keep making progress.

The Vietnamese language has a fairly simple structure. There are no tenses to the verbs, just words to indicate time—past, present, future. There are no articles either, so I had to learn to use them when they made no sense to me.

Chapter Four: Stay in the Present

English has many rules, and many exceptions to those rules. Those rules and exceptions have to be followed in order for the speaker to be understood. This made the language very difficult for me to learn.

It was an arduous process.

But I love language, and discovered I love English. Now that I am fluent in it I find it a very rich language. I love the precision of expression, the descriptive words. It is a gift to me as it conveys my thoughts and feelings so succinctly. I often told my husband, "I know I have so much to learn, but if I ever write a book, I will write in English."

Chapter Five: Be Disciplined and Fight the Good Fight

We were all learning to adapt to this new life, but of course it was vastly easier for our sons, and for our two daughters who were born here. Our children grew up as Asian Americans, bridging the chasm between their parents' Vietnamese culture and the American culture. They seemed to do it with ease while it was torturous for my husband and me.

As I continued to learn rudimentary English, I would look at my young children, wondering how I could guide and protect them in this strange country. I didn't know Western etiquette, customs, and morés. Everything I saw I knew I was viewing through the lens of my ignorance. It was terrifying and paralyzing, but my determination has always kept me looking for what I can do. Seeing the smallest shred of hope, of possibility, gives me the belief that I can get there, and I will keep going. I will find the way.

Education plays a major role in breaking down the wall of isolation for immigrants. Education opens the mind and eyes, and teaches how to communicate. It is a major key to opening the door to the opportunities and promise of this country.

Eventually, after a long talk with my husband, I enrolled in the ESL (English as a Second Language) class at the local community college.

Taking ESL classes helped to break down the social isolation I felt. The strange society I was in started to become less strange.

I continued to take courses at the community college and graduated with an Associate's Degree in Science.

The six years it took to get my associate's degree opened my mind and helped me connect with the world at large, and especially my new home and new culture. This opened up many opportunities for me that I wouldn't have had otherwise.

****

The way my father lived his life by example had a great effect on me. I wanted the example of my effort in gaining an education to demonstrate to my children the importance of education.

I felt, also, that I needed further education to be the mother I wanted to be: A great provider and a guiding light to my children. So I made a promise to myself that I would continue my education. That promise was unbreakable, no matter what I had to do.

My husband agreed that continuing my education was important and that he would work while I went to school at Illinois State University.

There were a few reasons for this. I was, after all, my father's daughter, and our family had an intellectual tradition. I was younger than my husband, energetic and eager to learn. I was also more comfortable in an educational environment.

My husband had come from a wealthy Chinese merchant family where education was not the focus, but the work ethic was highly prized. He worked incredibly hard and took care of many of the household chores and the children.

I was fascinated with economics and good with math, so I decided to go to school for economics and learn about business (I remembered what a good businessman my father was, I think business was in my blood).

****

While I attended school, Quang worked between 60 and 70 hours a week. During the week he worked as a housekeeper at the local hospital. On weekends he picked mushrooms at a mushroom farm and got paid by the basket. It might seem easy, but picking mushrooms is actually really hard work.

At home Quang did much of the cooking. He also watched the children a good deal of the time. Occasionally our sponsors hired a babysitter for a few hours to help with the kids so we could have a rest.

While I was attending university, Quang arranged his vacation times to coincide with my midterms and finals so he could care for the children while I concentrated on studying.

I have always been impressed and honored that he worked so hard without complaining.

****

For two years, three days a week, I would drive from La Salle to Normal, Illinois. The campus was seventy-five miles away and the trip took an hour-and-a-half each way.

The general guideline in college is that for every hour spent in class you should spend two hours studying. Not so for me! My ratio was one to six—six hours of studying for every hour of class. When I studied I had a stack of books near me: an English-Vietnamese dictionary, the *Oxford Dictionary of the English Language*, and textbooks for the class. When I looked up a word in the dictionary, if the definition had a word I didn't know, I'd have to look up the definition of that word, and if *that* definition had a word I didn't know, I'd look it up, and so on; it was a painstaking process.

I not only used the textbooks required for my classes but I would also check out other books from the library. They might be other books by the same author we were reading, or the same work but a different edition, or works by other authors. I slept an average of five hours a night, and when it was time for midterms and finals I only slept two to three hours at the most.

It took me 10 years from when I started school for English as a Second Language to when I got my bachelor's degree.

I wanted my example to instill in my children my work ethic, drive, motivation, energy, and determination. However, I didn't want my children to endure as much as I had in order for them to get a good education. After extensive research, in 1989, we decided to move to Massachusetts so that my children would be close to the best universities in the world.

In Massachusetts I worked for an insurance company. Knowing that over the next ten years I'd have four kids in college, I decided to get a second job. I worked as a cashier at a local grocery store evenings and weekends, putting my work total at sixty to seventy hours a week. My husband worked as a truck driver.

All of our children ended up going to top universities, and received the education I wanted them to have.

Education has been vital to my success: It broadened my knowledge and enlarged my soul and broke the wall of social isolation. It deepened my sense of my own value and the value of life. It helped me further embrace and respect life the way it is.

Our children have said that they got the expectation of going to school and excelling from me, and they got their strong work ethic from their father.

Chapter Six: Do Your Best, Be Honest...

"Do everything to the best of your ability, make an effort, bring energy and exude enthusiasm in all the things you do; live life to the fullest and make it significant. It comes down to: if you didn't get up tomorrow morning, who would miss you? What have you contributed in your life? What will you be remembered for?" Nguyen Van Tho

My father always stressed that I should do whatever I was doing to the best of my ability. He said "If you don't hit the finish line, you forfeit the chance to be a winner." So throughout my life whenever I start something I always finish it. I don't do anything half-way or leave it half-finished.

Wherever I worked, I was well-respected and appreciated. I always tried to see how I could do any job better. When I left a position, the job description would have changed, expanded by the responsibilities I had added to it.

I worked at a large insurance agency for twelve years. When I had a document for my boss to sign, he trusted me to have it done perfectly. Even though his signature was going to be on that document he knew he didn't need to check it over. He knew I had gone through it line by line, word by word, to catch any mistakes and make sure that it was exactly right.

Whatever I do I give 100 percent. I do it with pride, with enthusiasm, with grace and gratitude that I have the opportunity to do it. I do it

Chapter Six: Do Your Best, Be Honest…

wholeheartedly. If I tell someone I will do something, then they don't have to worry, because it will get done. I try to finish whatever I have promised to do ahead of schedule.

When I have done something to the best of my ability, if something goes wrong I will certainly regret it, but I won't feel a need to offer an apology for myself. I will know I have done all I could as well as I could.

My father often told me "You need to be one-faced. When you are honest, people appreciate it because they know they can count on you to tell the truth. When you tell a lie then you have to remember to keep up your story and it continues to build up and then even you won't know what the truth is."

****

When I was growing up my family had servants. One day my father found me scolding Mai, the girl who was my maid. He chastised me for my actions. He told me, "Say what you mean, mean what you say, but don't say it mean."

He was telling me to express my opinion with kindness and respect. It didn't matter to him who was being spoken to. He believed that everyone should be addressed respectfully. The truth can be told, and may need to be told, but it does not have to be conveyed in a mean-spirited or cruel fashion.

****

As my children were growing up I was more concerned about whether they were telling the truth than if they had done something to get in trouble. I encouraged them to come to me and be truthful. If they broke a vase, for example, if they were honest about it, no matter how valuable the vase was, I would say, "It's o.k., thank you for telling me. Accidents happen." I wanted to impress upon them that honesty is part of being a responsible, honorable person.

Being honest with yourself about your strengths and weaknesses lets you set goals that are reachable. When you don't know your strengths or your limitations, you have no way to gauge what is a reasonable expectation and what is not.

Honesty and clarity within yourself helps you know your limits and your strengths. You have a clear idea of what you can and can't do, what's reasonable. But beyond that, it allows you to then push beyond what you think your limits are, allows you to aim much higher and have a good chance of getting there.

So, remember to DREAM BIG!

Your dream, your vision, motivates you to move forward, and inspires you to go beyond your comfort zone. You need to dream big, make your vision enticing and grow yourself into the position where you want to be. Grow yourself by cultivating and nurturing your mind, through learning and continuing education and deliberate practice. Then you will be able to bring yourself to the level of success that you set your mind to.

****

I was always fascinated with the law. I wanted to be a lawyer and go to court and fight for the rights of those who could not fight for themselves. I saw myself in court presenting a case eloquently, persuasively, and compassionately. The case would be airtight because I had diligently researched every aspect of it. In my imagination I won many cases.

I had started law school in Viet Nam, and had to leave because of the war. But in the U.S., when I considered pursuing a career in law, the reality was that I had difficulty with the complexity of English. After an honest evaluation I believed that if I wanted to be a lawyer, I would eventually get there. However, because of my responsibility to my husband and children I didn't have the luxury of time or money to pursue such an ambitious endeavor. I studied economics instead.

Chapter Seven:
...and Keep Your Promises

When we arrived at Chicago's O'Hare Airport, we felt completely invisible. That feeling of invisibility and being utterly unable to communicate was the first time I promised myself I would learn English.

As we settled into our new life, I knew I needed to learn more English. I didn't want to be limited to just shopping for groceries and having simple everyday conversations. I had to be able understand the concerns in my community and the school my children were attending.

I wanted to be able to talk about what was going on in the world—understand *Meet the Press*, the economy and political points of view, express my take on the world around me. I wanted to engage in interesting, thought-provoking discussions.

Until I got a good grasp of the English language, I couldn't really share my feelings or voice my opinions with the people around me. Once, I was expressing my profound gratitude to my sponsors, telling them how deeply I appreciated what they had done for my family. I was speaking in Vietnamese. The translator listened to my heart-felt speech, turned to my sponsors, and said "She says, 'Thank you'."

Oh, I was so mad! I wanted to tell them how much their help had meant to us, but I just couldn't. I again promised myself that I would go to school and learn English. When one of our sponsors told me about the ESL program, I promptly enrolled.

My promise to myself and to my family, though they didn't know it, was to understand and speak English so I could truly communicate in my new language. Despite the difficulties in getting my ESL certificate, there was never any doubt in my mind that I would succeed. I had promised myself and that was it—my promise would be kept.

My father had told me, "A promise is a promise to keep and to deliver." Keeping the promises you make is very important in my Vietnamese culture and that of my father. You do not make a promise unless you know you can follow through with it.

My father said, "Rain comes down from the sky. It is the blessing that comes from above to below. My job is to take care of you, and your job is to take care of your children." I promised him that I would raise my children to become good, decent human beings—the way he had raised me to be. And of course I remembered what he had said—that when you are a parent, you parent your children until the day you die.

I took to heart my promise to raise my children well. When I dropped them off at school, I didn't say goodbye. Instead, I said, "Do your best, be honest, and keep your promises," just as my father had always said to me. I wanted those values to be ingrained in their subconscious, to always be there to guide them.

My promise to my children for their college education was that they would do their part and I would do my part. I said "You go to school, you get the grades, and apply to any college you want and if you get accepted we will see to it that you go there."

I didn't tell them that they could only apply to community or state colleges. I wanted them to go to any school they truly wanted, whether it was Harvard or Yale or a state college or university.

When my oldest son was accepted at Northeastern University, I was happy for him. But the financing was a problem. Because I wanted so badly for my kids to afford college, I was working that second job, and it put us just over the limit for financial aid.

I was not going to let this prevent my son from attending Northeastern: I had made a promise. I wrote to the director of the financial aid department and made my case to her personally. She assigned me to an associate director who was very kind and resourceful.

Because I was so determined and polite, while also putting our situation bluntly, we obtained the financial aid my son needed. When my second son was accepted at Northeastern also, the financial aid was put into place without a problem.

My word is my contract, honoring my commitment to myself and to others, no matter what. When you keep your promises, you don't know where they will take you next.

Chapter Eight: Let Your Vision Guide You, But Your Passion Lead You

"Live life with no regrets: let your vision guide you and your passion lead the way." My father's words are my compass. My passion is my GPS to help me navigate through life.

When I was young and inexperienced I thought I was the architect of my life, my future. I thought I could just plan my life out, and it would happen the way I had designed it.

As I've grown older and wiser, I now see myself more as a sculptor; to have the life I want I have to do a lot more than just designing. Every day I have to hammer, chisel, scrape, sculpt, and polish in order to shape my life into the form I want it to be.

Part of that sculpting work is cleaning up the mess. A sculptor has to clean up the stone chips, I have to clean up the messes of mistakes and everyday life, and pick up the pieces that fall off.

Occasionally I've thought the marble sculpture of my life was perfect, and then a piece has gotten knocked off. Then I've had to redesign and reshape the marble sculpture. But I've been so involved with my life as it moves forward that looking back in regret is not one of my options. I make the best out of what I have left. It changes the course of things, transforms them into a new shape. I have reinvented myself.

Chapter Eight: Let Your Vision Guide You, But Your Passion Lead You

I have reinvented myself at various times in my life, sometimes into a shape that is very different from what I ever imagined. I have often found myself being pushed out of my comfort zone. It is sometimes grueling work, and certainly scary, but also tremendously exciting.

You don't know what you can handle until you have been pushed past what you thought were your limits and you find you have not only survived but grown and thrived.

I don't have regrets because no matter how tough things have been, I've grown and stretched and found the excitement and joy of growing in my life.

****

The vision I've had for my life has always energized me, but the process to reach my visions—that is what really gives me wings. My passion ignites strong commitment and sustains my effort.

My vision of what I've wanted in my life is like a continuous dream. You get to one part of your life and the dream seems to have been realized, then you move forward and see that the dream continues.

It's like when you are traveling down a river and you come to a bend, you can only see a little distance. You have no way of knowing what you will find until you get there. Then you can see further and make plans for the next stage of the journey. The same is true of traveling over a mountain or going through a tunnel: you keep going until you reach the other side.

If you stop and give up before you get to where you want to be, you will never know what may have come your way just around the next corner, the next day, with the next push forward.

Traveling the river of my life has been a series of surprises as I've rounded the bends and found myself in new territory, facing new challenges and finding new delights.

****

Empowered by Hope

I knew the English-speaking professional world was hard to navigate for a woman who didn't speak English fluently. Although I wanted so much for my family, sometimes it seemed that even with my best efforts I couldn't get what I wanted. Others might have found reasons to give up, but failure and giving up were never options for me. I had a tough tenacity of purpose without which I would not have gone far.

I remember when I graduated from college, I had over two dozen interviews before I got hired for my first job. It was a frustrating experience because sometimes I had all the credentials, but I got rejection after rejection, and the unspoken message was that my English wasn't good enough.

****

When we left Vietnam, stealing away in the dead of night, we were gambling our lives for freedom. It was a deadly game of chance. Many of the Boat People who were trying to escape were not so lucky. They died or were captured by pirates. We were the lucky ones. We survived and overcame the daunting obstacles of the sea voyage. Our lives had been spared from violent storms, leaky sinking boats, and pirates.

At that point, surviving was the only thing that mattered.

Yet when the fact that we had survived had sunk in, then just being alive was not enough anymore. Now we were determined to live a full and significant life for the people who had sacrificed for us and for the terrible journey we'd been through. We wanted our lives to have meaning, to have something to show for the effort and to be able to give back for the help that had been given to us.

For many years my passion was taking care of my family and giving them a good life through improving myself and following my father's guidance.

All I have been through has given me the impetus to continue my efforts through whatever has come my way. That passion has given me joy in my accomplishments and what it took to achieve them.

I love to talk about my father, my children, my grandchildren. I enjoy telling the story of falling in love with my husband after 23 years of marriage. I love to coach. I want to share, not so much to teach, but to enlighten.

Chapter Eight: Let Your Vision Guide You, But Your Passion Lead You

My vision is to share my father's philosophy with people around the world. I have been given so much in this life. I want to give back to the world some of the blessings I have received. I humbly offer my gift and hope that people will accept and embrace it. My passion is in the sharing. I share my father's wonderful philosophy and the ways in which it was the foundation on which I built my life.

I have grown up quite a bit since I left my father's house. I have learned a lot; I have learned to respect and appreciate life as it is. I have learned that I have a very good life. Every night before I go to sleep and every morning I wake up with a deep sense of gratitude!

My father and I on my first trip back to Viet Nam, 1987

A Ha Moment:

Essays

A Ha Moment:

Happy New Year

I want to wish you a Happy New Year! May the New Year bring you plenty of Love, Luck, and Laughter!

How can you make sure that Love, Luck, and Laughter fill your coming year? According to my dad:

- First, you must expect that they—love, luck, and laughter—are coming your way.
- Second, you must clear the way and make room for them. If you are expecting these wonderful things to come into your life, you must clear out what is in the way and have space for them in your life. Be ready to welcome love, luck, and laughter into your life!
- Then, take a moment to appreciate their arrival and celebrate their presence. Embrace each moment of love, of luck, of laughter that comes your way and revel in the experience.

What Is Your New Year's Resolution?

I don't have one. I don't make New Year's resolutions. As far back as I can remember my dad never made any New Year's resolutions. However, two or three weeks before the New Year it was time for my father to reflect and do what he called "taking inventory."

He would revisit his goals for the year, a list of things to do/things that he wanted to accomplish. He had a very simple outline he used to sort out his goals by their importance:

Priority	Goals	Action Plan	Date	√
1				
2				
3				

He looked at the list of goals from the current year and saw which ones had been accomplished—those with a checkmark, and which ones hadn't—those without a checkmark.

The unchecked goals indicated that a specific goal fell short. Since the goal had not been reached, my father evaluated it carefully by asking:

- Why had it been so important to accomplish this goal?
- Why had it not been accomplished?
- What was holding him back, and why?
- Was it important enough to continue to pursue it?

If a goal was worth pursuing, then he kept the goal. Instead of giving up on it, or doing the same thing again that so far had not worked, he would do something different. He changed his strategy and his approach in order to reach that goal.

Setting Your Goals

Look at your goals for the year. Do you have a clear vision of what you want, and a well-defined and specific action plan for each goal?

Setting goals is very important. If you don't know where you are going, how will you know that you got there? Know your destination, know your purpose, know what you want to achieve…get set and Go!

Here are my criteria for setting your goals. They must:
- Be your own.
- Be big and compelling (just out of reach, but never out of sight).

And you must:

- Envision the outcome (Imagine you are already there—how do you feel? What does it look like, smell like, taste like? Look around you—is it as you imagine? Now, close your eyes and position yourself in this future place of accomplishment).
- Spell out your strategy: what needs to be done, and what are you doing to successfully implement your vision?
- Write down an action plan with specific goals. This shows you day-by-day where you are on the path with measurable, clear-cut actions and measurable results. (Use the table above as a template.).
- When it is done write down the date on your list and put a check mark there (celebrate your achievement). Ah, you've done it! Now you can see where you are on the journey to accomplishment.

Happy New Year and may you have the best year this year and every year!

A Ha Moment:

A Lost Love

The Vietnamese civil war was a long and exhausting affair, which claimed many lives and affected many families. In the 1970s my friends and I were teenagers. We had seen nothing yet of life or the world. This war was the bane of our existence. It destroyed our youth, our families, and our country. The war curtailed our innocent and carefree youth. It remains a haunting memory in our minds.

Many of my friends received the draft notice and reported for duty. Joining the army was mandatory.

****

It was a melancholy day; Luan, my high school sweetheart, had been drafted into the army. Family and friends gathered to say good-bye to him. His mother stood next to me with tears in her eyes, her hand holding mine. As we waved to him, her tears trickled down her aging cheeks. Luan was her youngest and only surviving son. She talked to me about Luan and her two sons who had already died in the war. I felt her heartbreak.

I remember the day Luan came home on leave, he was in mourning for his friend who had died in his arms on the battlefield. I was scared for him, for me and for his mother who already had two dead sons. He was so young and had already seen too much; I didn't know if he could handle it. And his mother and I were worried about whether he would live or die.

Silently, I walked next to him; he held my hand, but our silence spoke volumes. Without a word being said, I could feel his sadness and his pain, his fear, his despair. He was no longer the innocent boy I had said good-bye to. Now, his experience had moved him beyond my reach.

We stopped at Bado Café for a cup of coffee. The strong, black Vietnamese coffee dripped slowly from an individual coffee maker. Trinh Cong Son music, classical Vietnamese love songs, played softly in the background. He sat across from me, his elbows resting on the table. In his uniform and with a cigarette in his hand, I could not find the simplicity of his youth anywhere, I missed him already. I watched the cigarette smoke embrace his face, he looked tired and dispirited. I could see him drowning in sadness.

It had rained earlier and every time the wind blew, more leaves fell. The bareness of autumn made it so dreadful. Again, I strolled along next to him, my hand in his. His voice was cold and distinct and melancholy: "The leaves fall from the trees, just like our soldiers fall in the battle field, rudely unrecognized!" I cried. From the depth of my soul, I cried for those unknown, unrecognized soldiers.

On October 23, 1974, Luan and his troops were ambushed and they were forced to surrender. When I heard the news, I was horrified. The day was cold and drizzly, and this dreadful news made it seem much longer then twenty-four hours.

I was listening to the radio for the news, but because of the long-winded reporter and the noisy crowd around me, along with my accelerating heartbeats, I did not comprehend what had just happened. I was asking people around me "Please, someone tell me what is going on." I was in anguish, desperate to know what had actually happened and where. Maybe Luan hadn't been affected.

Later, I found out that Luan had been wounded and was being treated in Nha Trang military hospital.

I went with two of my friends to visit Luan in the hospital. His mother was there, completely gray, aged from agony and sorrow, sobbing, "Go home, Ha! He doesn't want to see you."

I was dismayed and confused as I felt my heart breaking. Why didn't he want to see me? I thought he would be so excited to see me, his love. It didn't make any sense.

Then I saw him! I pulled the curtain aside and just peeked in at him. He was lying there. Emotionless and motionless, his left leg had been amputated. At that moment I knew I had lost him forever.

He was such a proud man; he wouldn't have wanted me to feel sorry for him. And he would have felt that he had nothing left to offer me. He never told me these things, but I knew him so well, there was no need.

I left the hospital. I felt alone, the loneliness and sorrow deeply seated in my heart. Grief consumed me.

I never saw him again.

I lost much in the war. My first love was one of the casualties.

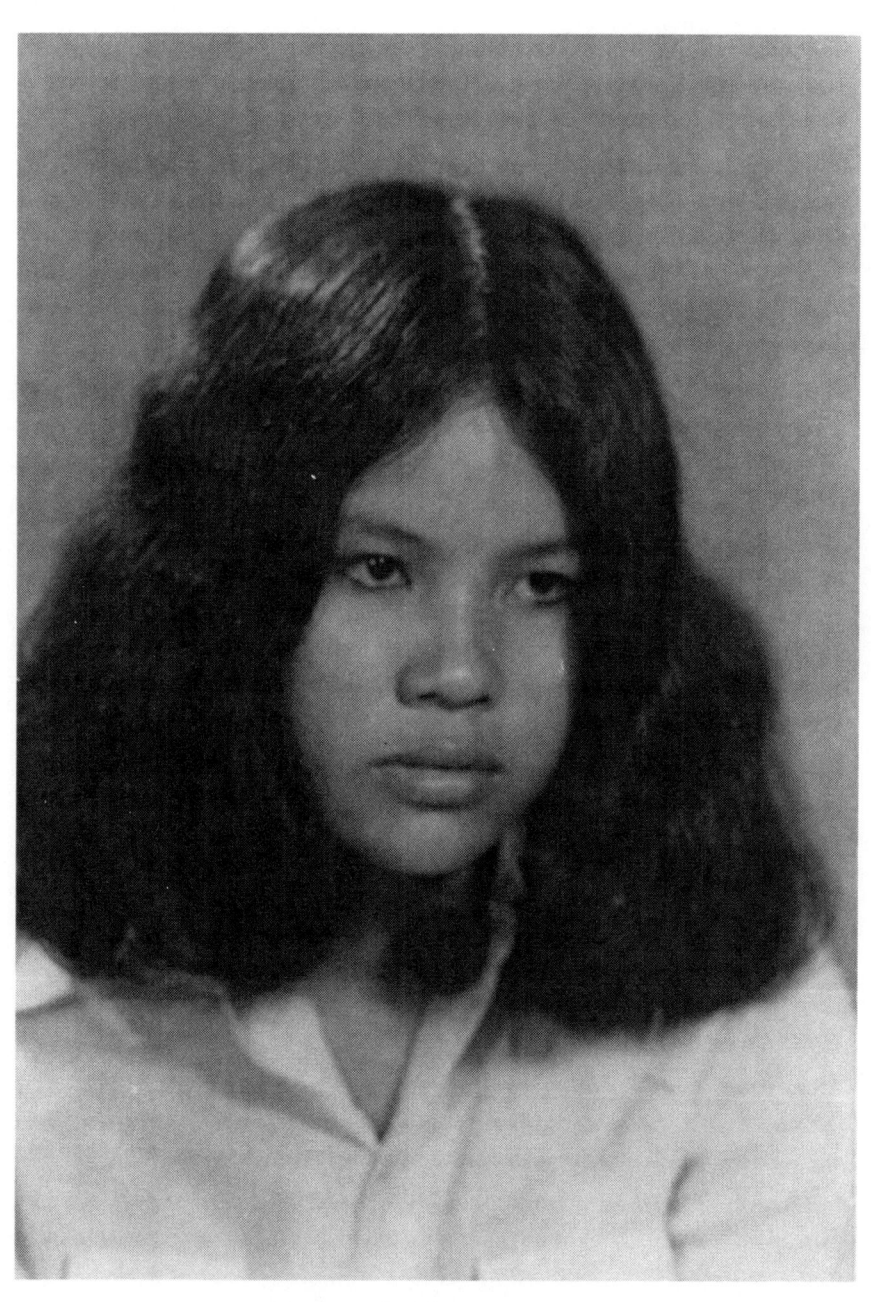

*Nguyen Thi Thu Ha in 1975,
a twenty year old facing an uncertain future*

A Ha Moment:

What Price Freedom?

What is freedom? What does freedom mean to you? What price are you willing to pay in order to obtain freedom? To me it's priceless: It means being able to make my life what I want it to be, with sacrifice, courage, faith, and hope.

The Vietnamese civil war was a long and exhausting affair, which claimed many lives and affected many families, both Vietnamese and American.

In the 1970s I was a teenager. I had seen nothing yet of life and the world. My father was a very successful businessman so I grew up with luxury and privilege, everything I wanted my father would give me. I never had to struggle for anything I wanted or needed, it was simply handed to me.

When I was growing up, I was unaware of the civil war. It had been going on since I was very young, and had not yet affected me. The Tet Offensive in 1968 brought the war into my consciousness.

The Easter Offensive of 1972 escalated the war, and many of my friends were drafted as they finished high school. At that point I really started to understand the ramifications of the war.

The war wreaked havoc on my life. It curtailed the innocent and carefree days of my youth, and destroyed many of our young people, their families, and my country. It still haunts me; it is always an undercurrent in my mind

April 30, 1975. That was the day when South Vietnam fell to the Communists. I was hiding in a shelter underground and afraid I would die. Life as I had known it had just become a distant memory.

The atmosphere in Vietnam under the Communists at that time was one of fear and terror. Everyone spied on everyone else, and if you did something someone didn't like, you could be reported to the authorities. We were constantly at risk of offending the wrong person, doing the wrong thing. Anyone could be arrested and tortured at any time.

Being wealthy was now a liability, and my father could no longer work at his business. The new government considered him an oppressor of the people, thinking that he was forcing them to work for him without proper recompense. We were paralyzed with fear and anticipation of horrible things, and within a few months we were put in a re-education camp.

When we got out, my father was forced to make one of the most difficult decisions of his life. To ensure my safety and survival he knew I must escape the Communist regime and leave Vietnam, the only home I had known.

My faith and my strength carried me through to be able to know what freedom was about, in a way that was wholly new to me. I appreciate freedom today far more than I could have if I had not had to struggle and sacrifice for every bit of the life I have now.

*May 1, 1987: We achieved the freedom we sought
and became citizens of the United States*

A Ha Moment:

Obstacles

My husband and I came to America from Vietnam. We had many obstacles to overcome. Our complications consisted of a language barrier, culture shock, and raising Asian American children in a culture that was foreign to us.

The language barrier really impaired our ability to function in the day-to-day world of this new culture. We did not say much of anything because it was very difficult for us to express ourselves. When we did speak, we often spoke with our hands and used lots of facial expressions to try to convey our meaning. We must have looked like demented mimes!

We were two intelligent adults who were very capable of making decisions based on reason and logic, but we allowed ourselves to make decisions based instead on gut feelings and fear. It was very difficult for us; our prospects seemed grim at the time, and our future felt really uncertain.

My husband constantly reminded me of what his father had told him throughout his childhood: "If you cannot say anything profound, then do not say anything at all. Observe and learn." He was poking fun at us, because we couldn't speak in this new language at all! So Quang said that we were certainly in the right position to observe and learn.

We had two, and eventually four, children depending on us, and we couldn't see how we were going to guide them and give them the life we had come to this country to give them. It was painful to feel so bewildered and helpless.

We were struck and dismayed by the boldness and beauty of American culture. Americans were so much more outspoken and casually friendly than our culture in Vietnam. It was a learning curve, adjusting through our culture shock to understand American society. It was good that our children were so young, because they grew up in this culture and didn't have to learn to adapt the way my husband and I did.

Before they began going to school the language and culture differences were difficult, but manageable. Our world was fairly small and we could navigate in it. We were able to live by our Vietnamese customs and values, without a lot of interference from the outside world.

However, that all changed when the children began going to school. Now they were exposed to American culture and values, and a gulf opened up between them and their father. He was very set in his ways, and at that point he had no intention of changing.

My husband didn't want to let go of the traditions that he so dearly protected. He wanted to live in America as he had in Vietnam. He embraced his culture: "I lost everything in my quest for freedom—my traditions, my culture, and my values. Let me hold on to them."

He had tremendous conflicts with our children. In his culture, a child absolutely obeyed his parent without question. It was different from the way kids are raised here! Our children would challenge his authority and decisions. This really upset and hurt him. He would roar like a wounded panther.

Throughout their childhood, the unwanted battles continued, the stupendous struggles of an emotional war that no one wins, but all get caught in its maddening crossfire. I found myself trying to make peace between my husband and my children, but there was no understanding from any of them. I felt like I was fighting an uphill battle. It was tough on everyone.

So our children grew up as Asian Americans. They were immersed in American culture, and developed their own identities as individuals in their communities.

My husband, however, is a man of China. I call him that because even though he was born and raised in Vietnam, he was the oldest son of a Chinese family, and he grew up with Chinese values in his bones.

My husband has good intentions but he is stubborn and resistant to change; therefore, it was very difficult for him to let go. He would prefer that our children still be at the age when they accepted and obeyed him, rather than challenge his authority.

He always obeyed his father without question, even when he became an adult, and he expects his children to obey him the same way. This makes it really difficult for them to have a harmonious relationship.

I often remind our children who we were and where we came from. I told them they must always acknowledge that their father is a Chinese man with many complications and many obstacles he had to overcome. He is a man of China who raised Asian American children.

My husband and I have reverence for both our old and new cultures. We are gratified that we did the best job we knew how in raising our children in such conflicting worlds. Our journey continues. I often contemplate how far we have come!

My husband Quang Tran on his first trip back to Viet Nam in 1984.

A Ha Moment:

From the Mouths of Babes

This past week-end, I had a great time visiting with friends. We enjoyed the gift of each other's company and an extraordinarily fine lunch.

We had first met thirty years ago. At the time our children were toddlers, and now, our children are parents themselves. Time just flies! My friends brought their granddaughter and I brought my album full of pictures of my beautiful grandchildren. First we caught up on our children—their three children and my four. Then we talked about the good old days and then, of course, we exchanged anecdotes about our grandchildren and the innocent and magical age they are right now.

I told them how impressed I am with my two sons and their wives and their son and his wife…What good parents they all are. The way they care for their children, discipline them…Ah, I think they are much better equipped to be great parents then we were.

One of the great joys of being a grandparent is that we can just enjoy the grandchildren, then hand them back to their parents. Because our children are themselves such good parents, we can happily return our precious grandchildren to them.

Life is good. However, the fact remains that we are getting older. My friends gently reminded me: Yes, we are getting old! But that means we still have a wonderful life to live with the newest generation.

****

Life is full of surprises and at times, despite how hard you try to move ahead, you just feel like you're on a treadmill. You're going the distance but not getting anywhere, you're still in the exact same spot! Sometimes we feel like we're juggling many balls, putting in lots of effort just to keep them in the air, without accomplishing anything. At these times we feel overwhelmed, frustrated, out-of-control.

In the black hole of frustration and despair, there is a magnetic force that can suck you in, so you need to find a way to move out of reach of that magnetic suction. How do you resist it and get moving again?

Okay, take a deep breath. Find your center, the part of you that is calm and quiet (yes, you know it's there *somewhere*) and feel the strength of your inner balance.

You may need to take a few minutes, or an hour or a day, to sit with your calm, balanced self and rest and bring your focus back to the present, to what is most important. Decide what really needs to be done now, and what can wait till later. Can you ask for help, delegate a bit? Just let some of it go? Whatever you decide, you will have an easier, more productive time after you have centered and focused yourself.

I learned this lesson recently from my three-year-old granddaughter, my esteemed "old" philosopher. In the midst of spinning out of control, too many things to do and too little time to do it, she taught me a profound lesson in living everyday life.

Going into the bathroom, she told me that she's a big girl now; she doesn't have to sit on the Elmo booster toilet seat any more. "See A'Má! I just balance myself so that I don't fall into the big bowl." And that's what she did!

I had my own "A Ha" moment then…the key is balance.

As I said when I parted from my friends, until we meet again, my friends, I wish you good health, good fortune, and a good sense of equanimity.

I have great pride in myself for what I have accomplished. I see how worthwhile the struggle was when I see how well all my children are doing in this new homeland. The obstacles I climbed over to get here were huge, but they gave me a strength and appreciation that I would not have otherwise.

Our family continued to grow in 2006 with our first grandchild, Ella Kha Lien Tran

We welcomed our first grandson in July 2007
Davis Shimizu Tran

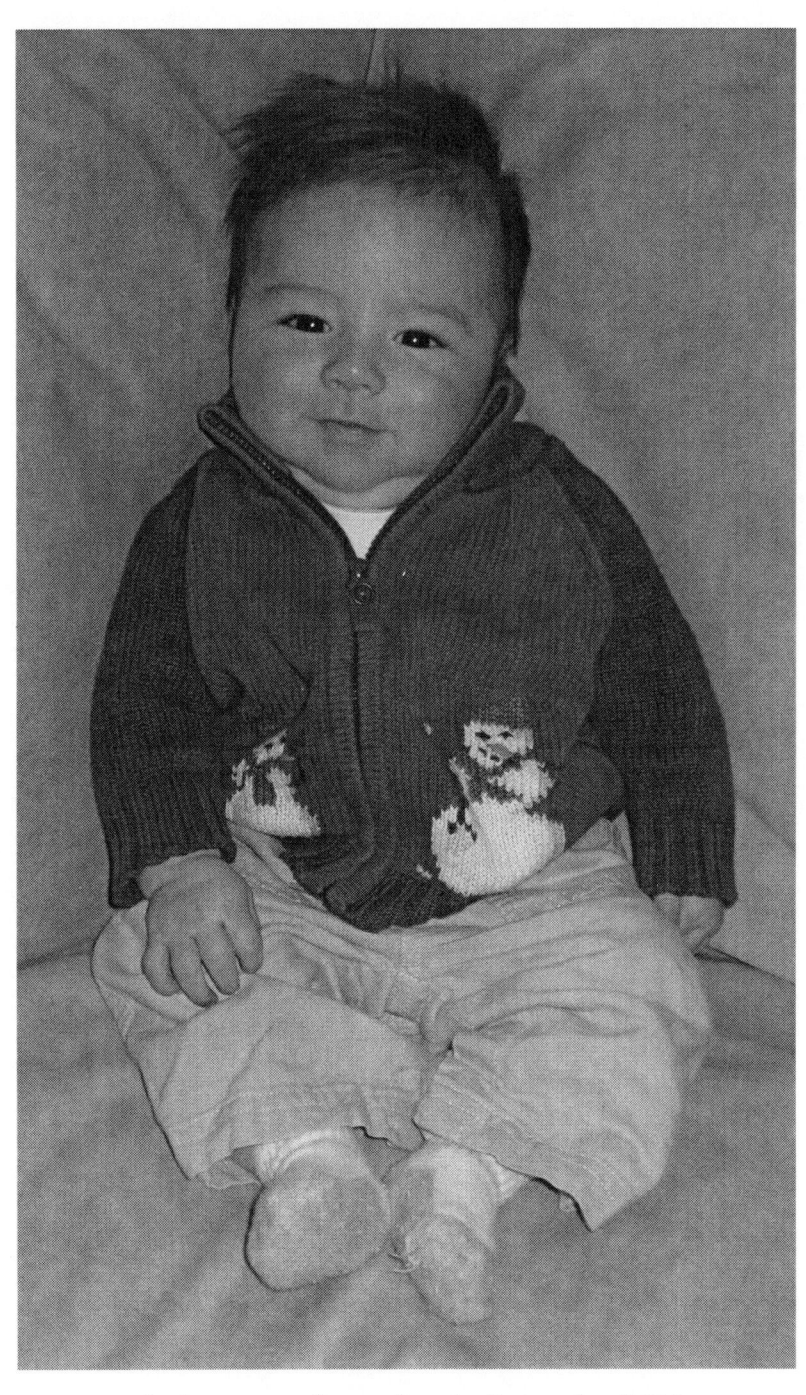

And our second grandson in September 2008
Caden Thieu Tran

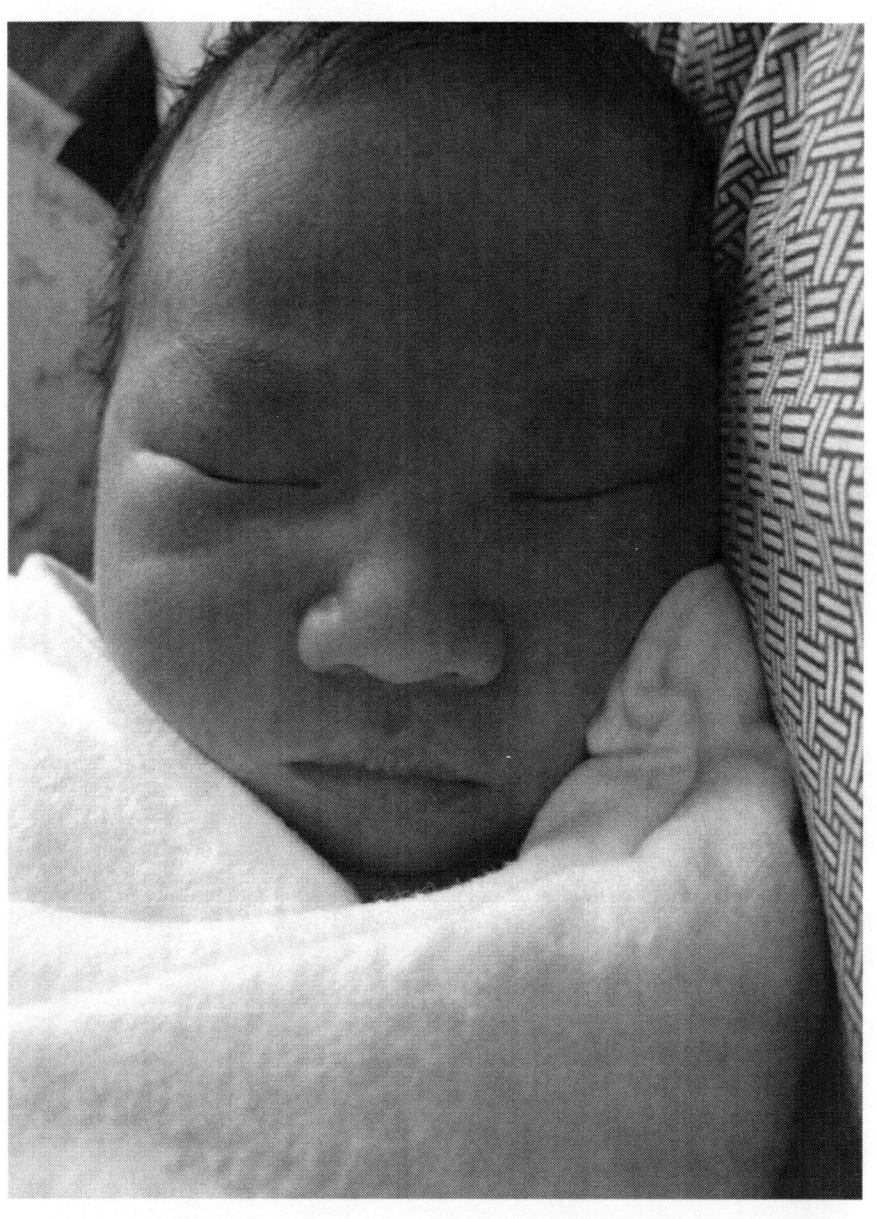

The most recent addition to our family arrived in January 2010
Spencer Shimizu Tran

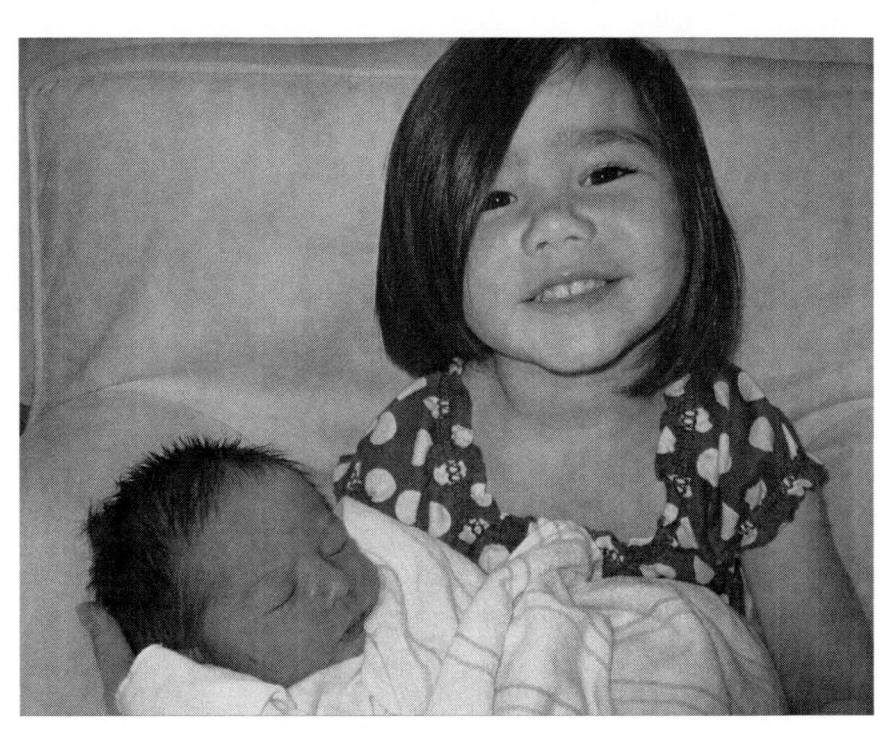

Ella loves the role of big sister to Caden

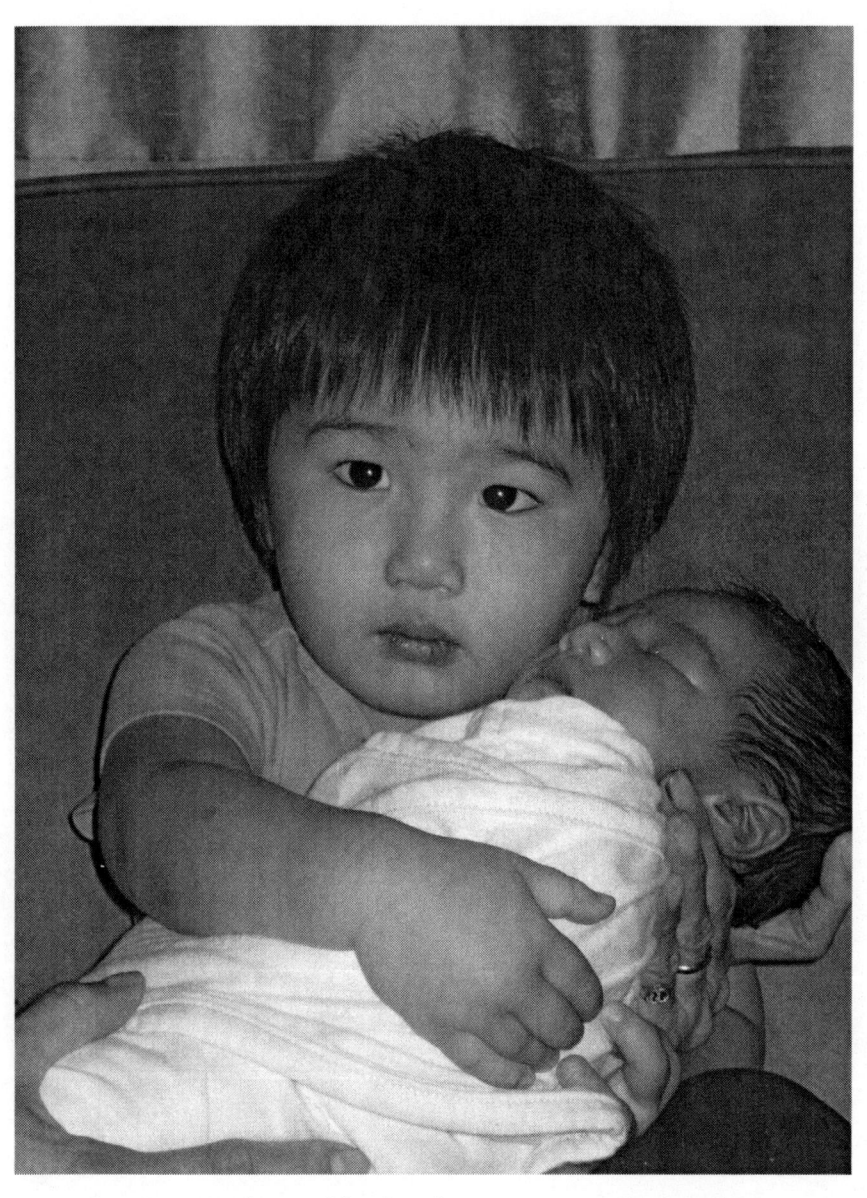

Davis welcomed his brother Spencer to the family

Letters from the Heart

A Father's Day Dedication to My Dad, June 2009

"Do everything to the best of your ability, make an effort, bring energy and exude enthusiasm to all the things you do; live life to the fullest and make it significant. It comes down to: if you didn't get up tomorrow morning, who would miss you? What have you contributed in your life? What will you be remembered for?" Nguyen Van Tho

Father's Day is coming up, and even more than usual, I'm thinking about my dad. He's living in Vietnam, and I haven't seen him in five years—far too long. I will see him in November and my heart is bursting with anticipation.

I decided long ago I would do nothing in my life that did not reflect positively on my father's life. My father didn't tell me how to live. He just lived and let me watch. His actions spoke volumes, and his words held weight because they were backed by his actions.

My journey has been a long, tough, and often rough road. Coming from Vietnam to this new country was a gift but also presented many difficulties. When I was here, despite the obstacles, I was determined to enjoy my freedom, to pursue a good quality of life for my family, and to honor both my old and new cultures. However, working so hard for my family, many times I felt that I had no more energy to keep going. Those were the times when I would remember what my father had told me.

His words were a gift I had not realized were with me. When I got discouraged, I looked inside myself for something to keep me going. I *heard* my father's voice in my head: "Keep living your life until you draw your last breath." It was as if he had encoded his voice onto a computer chip and embedded it in my brain's memory bank.

All the times during my childhood that he had repeated his philosophical sayings over and over had had a miraculous power to keep me going. When I was at my lowest points, I remembered what he said and found the love and strength to continue.

I missed my father so much when I came to this country and I wanted him still to be able to care for me. Though he hasn't been here with me, he gave me the gift of his philosophy, and to this day it continues to carry me forward.

These sayings became the foundation I have used to propel myself forward and achieve my dreams. They are priceless gifts I appreciate and will treasure for the rest of my life. In fact I have used these gifts to teach my children.

In remembering what my father said and putting his philosophy into practice I discovered what his words meant and how they apply to my life in the present.

By sharing my father's philosophy, I honor him and what he sacrificed for me, and I ensure that his wisdom lives on in those who carry it forward. I believe this is a timeless, universal philosophy of use to everyone.

On this Father's Day, I want to express my profound gratitude to my dad, for he is love personified. Dad, you are the brightest star shining in the galaxy, taking me upward as I follow you. You are my compass in life! Your wisdom enlightens and inspires me. I have found over the years that your thoughts and dreams have inspired and enriched all the people's lives you have touched. I am honored to be your daughter.

My children will wonder why I wrote a letter to only one son, and not one to each of them. It's not because I love any of them less. It is simply the circumstances of his birth and babyhood that created a bond that is different from the one I share with my other children. I hope that they will understand better when they have read this.

A Letter to My Son, Calvin

My dearest son,

Today is your 26th birthday. Every day of your life you give me a gift of being who you are and who you have become.

As I write to you, I am engulfed by the memory of the first day we met. The midwife placed you in my arms; I remember how proud and happy I was. You were a beautiful baby boy, my baby. You mesmerized me with your presence. Your eyes were closed, your mouth yawned open. You opened your hands and stretched your arms and legs, and then you went back to sleep. I rocked you gently in my arms. Time was standing still.

When you were twenty-eight days old, the guide for the "Boat People" contacted us—at long last, time for us to leave. Our journey began at that moment.

The man came to our hut and signaled for us to follow him. Your dad carried your brother and I carried you. We followed the unknown man to an unknown location. In the dark, moonless night the wind whispered in the dry air. We walked through dried grass, and then the hard, sharp stubble of the rice patties. My heart drummed accelerating anxious beats. My ankle was throbbing with excruciating pain, from when it got broken the day you were born.

I dragged my injured leg while I was clutching you tightly in one arm. I struggled painfully to continue—you motivated me. You did not make a sound. You seemed to understand the importance and necessity of your silence.

I held you closer to my heart to assure you that I was there with you. But you must have known already the solemn promise from my heart: I was there from the first day of your existence and always will be there.

I was very sick on the boat. You were in my arms. After a day with no food or water, my milk supply dried up. It still hurts me to remember how you cried for nourishment and I had none to give you. You cried and cried until you were so exhausted you slept.

After less then three days at sea, the captain announced that the boat engine had ceased working. You cannot imagine what a chaos that was. People were screaming, children were crying. But you weren't. I cradled you in my arms. I closed my eyes and I prayed to Buddha, to my deceased mother, who was watching over us. The old fishing boat was drifting to sea. I was unconscious from dehydration.

A soft touch on my shoulder, I opened my eyes to see a woman kneeling beside me. She was draped in white and, helping me sit up, she wrapped a blanket around my shoulders. She spoke to me in a soft voice, in a language that I did not understand. Oh God! I had died and gone to heaven. I had broken my promise to you and to your brother...forgive me.

As I prepared for my case in Heaven—I was not heaven-worthy because I had failed my sons and therefore I must be sent back to make it right—another woman dressed in the very same fashion, all in white, came toward me and presented me with a bundle in her arms. It was you! You were sleeping comfortably in a soft blue blanket. Your breath and your fresh scent were just like spring air on an April morning. I was immensely relieved. You were in my arms. Life was precious and being alive was wonderful.

Later, I learned that those women were nuns on board of a rescue boat that had picked us up and brought us to an island in Malaysia.

However, in my own mind they remain my angels, whether on earth or in heaven it makes no difference to me. I am indebted to them. I believed, then and always, that somewhere out there someone watched over us.

*Another ending, another beginning: dancing with
my son Dinh at his wedding in 2004*

Proudly standing with my son Do at his wedding in 2007, as he begins life as a husband

Words Of Wisdom From Sam Antion

I have been blessed with so many gifts from my father, some of which I have shared here with you.

I have also been blessed with people I have met along the path of bringing this work to life.

I have had a rare opportunity to talk with many who have shared with me the gifts they received from their fathers. One person, who may be known to many of you, is Tom Antion. We had an opportunity to talk at length and he shared with me the wisdom he received from his father.

Tom graciously offered to allow me to share with you one of his father's gifts, in the form of the leadership skills that were passed to him. Now they are yours as well. From all of us, Tom, thank you and your dad for this gift. I am certain it will inspire others as it has both of us.

****

Tom Antion and Associates Communication Company provides entertaining and informative keynote speeches and educational seminars, from advanced public speaking and presentation skills training to high-end Internet marketing training for small business. Tom is the author of the best selling presentation skills book *Wake 'em Up Business Presentations.* **And** *Click: The Ultimate Guide to Electronic Marketing.*

Leadership Skills from My Dad

Tom Antion

I've been bragging about my dad ever since 1973, when I did my high school graduation speech. I've even done professional speeches about one of the techniques he used to make me tough when I was just a baby.

Until I was preparing his eulogy, I had never actually written down all the leadership skills he taught me. As I was working on them, I thought that they would be a good example that anyone can use, both in their lives and from the speakers' platform.

I only saw Dad speak in public once and that was at his 50th wedding anniversary, but I witnessed his leadership skills my whole life.

Here's my list of Sam Antion's Top 10 Leadership Skills.

Leadership Skill # 1
BUILD IT STRONG

Dad would always build things more sturdily than they needed to be so that he never had to worry when extraordinary force was applied. He knew that whatever he built would stand up to the test. This applied to both character traits and real hammer-and-nail construction.

In fact, without his insistence on this leadership trait, I would not be here today.

When I was 16 years old a drunk driver doing nearly 100 mph ran his car off the road and smashed it into the corner of our living room. I was the only one in the room when it exploded around me. Had this been a normally built house, the car would have burst through the wall and killed me.

Leadership Skill # 2
DON'T TAKE SHORT CUTS

Dad was an electrician by trade. When doing his wiring he would always route the flat wires he worked with in a nice, symmetrical, and evenly spaced pattern. He would never just cut across the shortest distance to save wire and make his costs a little cheaper.

I remember as a child watching him and asking him why he did this when it would be a lot shorter to just run the wires directly between two points. He said, "When someone looks at this job years from now they will know that a professional did it and also, if they ever have trouble, they will be able to track down the problem easier because I did a nice, neat job."

I can't remember dad ever being out of work one day in my whole life. When everyone else was laid-off, he was always in demand.

Leadership Skill # 3
DON'T WASTE THINGS OR PEOPLE

Think a rock isn't worth much? Read on.

At the age of 73 Dad was purchasing some used lumber that someone had advertised in the paper. When he went to pick it up he saw a large number of boulders in the front yard of the place where he bought the lumber. He asked what they were going to do with the boulders. The man said, "I just want to get them out of here." Dad spent two weeks hauling them back to our house and another two months cutting them up with a chisel and a hammer. He then built a beautiful stone fireplace and chimney for one of our rental properties.

Also, I can't tell you the number of nails I removed from used lumber that dad made me straighten and use over again. I still do it to this day. A bent nail with a little help can be very useful again.

Sometimes people also need a little help to do the job they were meant to do.

Leadership Skill # 4
BE SELF-RELIANT

Working as a team is great, but when the team isn't there you just don't sit down and wait for help. Dad built pretty much every building and rental property we owned. I remember being so busy with football and other activities that I didn't get to help him too much (I probably would have slowed him down anyway).

One day while he was working on remodeling one of our buildings he asked me to go to the automotive parts store to get him about 20 feet of clear gas line tubing and several bottles of Coca Cola. I wondered what he was up to because he never drank Coke and our car was working fine.

I came back with the tubing and the Coke and stood back and watched as he did his thing. He plugged one end of the tubing and started pouring Coke in the other end (I was sure he had lost his mind after spending three months building the chimney). He said, "When you boys aren't around it's hard for me to make things level because I can't be at both ends of these long 2x4s. So I'm going to nail one end of this tubing on one end of where I'm working and take the other end of the tubing with me to the other end of the board."

He knew from his physics studies that liquids seek their own level. He could see through the clear tubing to the Coca Cola inside. The level of the Coke on one end of the tubing would be exactly the same level as at the other end of the tubing and that's where he would nail his board and it was always perfectly level.

Leadership Skill # 5
STUDY

Dad only went to the 5th grade and that was after skipping two grades, so he really only had three years of formal education. At ten years old (he was the oldest boy in a family with a deceased father) he was head of his household and shining shoes to support the family. He saved part of his tips and ordered an electrical engineering course from the American School.

At 13 he had his own electrical contracting company and installed the first electric light in Carnegie, PA. He also bought his younger sister the first electric washing tub in Bridgeville, PA.

He would read, read, and read some more every time he wanted to learn how to do something. When he retired around the age of 73 he sat down and read the ENTIRE *World Book Encyclopedia*. Now that's a lot of reading!

Being legally blind at age 94, he still listened to hours and hours of biographies and books on tape, and newspapers on tape, provided by the Library of Congress for blind people. He knew more about current events than anyone.

If you want to learn how to do something, study and try it out until you get it right.

Leadership Skill #6
YOU CAN HAVE WHATEVER YOU WANT IF YOU ARE WILLING TO WORK FOR IT

This was the 1910 version of "Just do it."

I don't want you to think I wasn't given tons of things by my parents, because I was. But the most valuable thing they gave me was being conditioned from a very young age that the world didn't "owe" me a living. I had to earn it.

I got a serious work ethic that I will always carry with me. If I want something, I go after it. I won't step on people to get whatever it is, and I won't cheat or steal, but I will work until I get it or don't want it anymore.

This would be a foreign language to many of today's youth.

Leadership Skill #7
GIVE BEFORE YOU GET

During the Depression work was more than scarce . . . more like non-existent. Even my dad was out of work. He told me that he said to himself, "I'm a really valuable worker and I'm not going to sit around here and do nothing when there is work out there to be done." He knew there was a fruit shipping warehouse not too far from where he lived so he went down to the loading docks dressed for work and just started helping the men load apples. Eventually the foreman noticed him and asked the other guys who he was. They said they didn't know but that he just started loading apples.

In fact, he was doing the work of three men. The foreman was so impressed he hired him on the spot and he hired several of my dad's cousins who were willing to prove themselves first.

Not realizing I was being influenced by my dad, I used to do the same thing when my landlord in college would work on our house. I would go out and help him just to learn how to fix things. This same landlord gave me the biggest financial break of my young career. When he retired to Florida, he sold me his largest rental property and guaranteed the financing himself. I hadn't even graduated from college yet!

Leadership Skill #8
YOU CAN OVERCOME OBSTACLES

This is one of my favorites. I have a visual that I use in a segment of a program called "You Are Unstoppable." The visual depicts a baby crawling on cushions with a red ball on the other side of the cushions.

Dad told me that when I was a baby, he would put my toys on one side of the room and put pillows in front of me to teach me to overcome obstacles. Anyone who knows me sees all the time that I'll figure a way to get something done if it is worthwhile.

Knowing that you can't be held back no matter what happens to you is a very powerful feeling to have inside. It gives you an unbridled confidence. Both my parents aligned to make me feel this way.

Most of you don't know this about me, but 14 years ago I lost everything and was totally broke. I was sleeping on a mattress in a vacant house, injured and unable to walk, and living off credit cards. The powerful feeling burned inside of me to overcome this obstacle. I did this by coming up with an idea for a unique entertainment company that in turn helped launch my speaking career.

Leadership Skill # 9
STICK BY YOUR SPOUSE

Well, I haven't had much chance to try this one out yet, but when I do get the chance . . . I will.

Words Of Wisdom From Sam Antion

My dad stuck by my mother even when, as a know-it-all teenager, I knew she was clearly wrong. Maybe that's why they made it 57-plus years. (I'll have more to say on this one if I ever get some real-life experience.)

Leadership Skill # 10
RISK EVERYTHING FOR SOMETHING REALLY WORTHWHILE

Did you ever wonder why so many people don't achieve their goals? Could it be because they were never really willing to commit fully to them? . . . They always gave themselves easy outs so if the going got tough they could bail out easily.

Around 1946, with a house full of kids and more on the way, Dad took every nickel he had, went 50 miles outside of the city and bought 156 acres of land, a bull-dozer and enough fuel to run it. He did not want his kids being raised in the filthy air and tough streets of Pittsburgh, PA.

He built a truck stop and motel and eventually warehouses, rental cottages, and our house on National Route 40 one mile east of Claysville, PA. His work can still be seen there today.

All the kids grew up healthy and strong and not one ever got into any trouble (except the time I ran away from home and ate grass soup and hot dogs for two hours before I gave up and returned home).

****

Even though my Dad was only on stage once that I know of, his leadership principles are influencing tens of thousands of people through me and because of all the people he touched over the years.

I spent the 4th of July this week at the funeral home viewing which, to be honest, I thought was going to be a pretty barren site, especially because at his age all his friends had died off. I couldn't believe it—people were everywhere! People that I'd never seen before or even heard of were telling me stories of when they were down and out 60 or even 70 years ago, and my dad was the one who helped them, or gave them a chance, or encouraged them.

I just about fell on the floor when someone told me that around 1923 my dad took on the responsibility for an entire family of kids who had an old drunk for a father. Dad worked all week for 50 cents to buy a big sack of potatoes to feed six kids and himself for the week. I was told that Dad taught the boys of the family trades so they could go out and find work and that these people thought the sun rose and set on my Dad. I had never heard a word about them before my Dad's viewing.

Oh, one more lesson that maybe I didn't learn too well from Dad—don't boast, just do good things.

WHAT'S THIS GOT TO DO WITH GREAT SPEAKING, TOM?

Well, I'm hoping if you've read this far that you've seen some value in my Dad's leadership teachings. I'm hoping that when you take the stage you walk up there as a good example for the many people you will touch in your career.

My Dad didn't have the stage in the conventional sense the way we do every time we speak. He "lived" the stage. In fact, he "was" the stage that good leadership stands on.

Your living example both on the stage and off will be what ultimately makes you a "Great Speaker." I can teach you the techniques, but you must provide the good example 24 hours a day/seven days a week. . . not just when you are on the platform.

Thanks Dad,

Love,

Your little "Heapy"

SPEAKERS: Feel free to use any of the examples you see in this essay. Even if you just substitute the term "this old man I heard of" for Sam Antion, that's OK. His leadership legacy will live on.

Hope: Inspirational Quotes

Patience is the art of hoping.
-Vauvenargues

Hope is faith holding out its hand in the dark.
-George Lies

Hope is the positive mode of awaiting the future.
-Emil Brunner

Desire + Expectation = Hope = A new take on life.
-Ha Tran

I always entertain great hopes.
-Robert Frost

Hope is one of those things in life you cannot do without.
Leroy Douglas

Refusal to hope is nothing more than a decision to die.
Bernie S. Siegel

We should not let our fears hold us back from pursuing our hopes.
- John F. Kennedy

*We want to create hope for the person ...
we must give hope, always hope.*
- Mother Teresa

Without hope men are only half alive. With hope they dream and think and work.
- Charles Sawyer

The important thing is not that we can live on hope alone, but that life is not worth living without it.
-Harvey Milk

It has never been, and never will be, easy work! But the road that is built in hope is more pleasant to the traveler than the road built in despair, even though they both lead to the same destination.
- Marion Zimmer Bradley

Optimism is the faith that leads to achievement. Nothing can be done without hope or confidence.
- Helen Keller

Hope is the anchor of the soul, the stimulus to action, and the incentive to achievement.
- Unknown

Extreme hopes are born of extreme misery.
- Bertrand Russell

Every area of trouble gives out a ray of hope, and the one unchangeable certainty is that nothing is certain or unchangeable.
- John F. Kennedy

Hope is an adventure, a going forward, a confident search for a rewarding life.
- Dr. Karl Menninger

Hope...is not a feeling; it is something you do.
Katherine Paterson

Of all the forces that make for a better world, none is so powerful as hope. With hope, one can think, one can work, one can dream. If you have hope, you have everything.
-Unknown

Once you choose hope, anything's possible.
- Christopher Reeve

To get a copy of my free e-book "The 1001 Inspirational Quotes & Then Some" please visit my blog: www.hope-empowered.com

Coaching/Mentoring

"To realize your dreams you must have a clear vision, a commitment, a strategy, and engage in action." Ha Tran

ARE YOU READY FOR A CHANGE?

Thinking about making changes in your life, career or business, but not sure how to do it?

WORKING WITH A CERTIFIED COACH CAN MAKE THE DIFFERENCE.

You will receive the personalized coaching that you have been seeking:

- To stay on top of your vision and direction
- To learn how to develop good habits and throw out the negative shadows
- To gain clarity in your life—personal or professional or both
- To be challenged to go beyond where you believe you can go
- To create an action plan that suits your life with the support and assistance of someone who believes in you

The work we will do includes:

- Self evaluation to determine your strengths and downfalls
- Revisiting what's holding you back and how to get beyond those hurdles
- Actions designed to bolster and build your self esteem
- Examination of your now environment/your today landscape
- Definition of where you want to go, your end game
- Accountability: You will learn how to focus and stay on course until completion of each step (FOCUS: Follow One Course Until Success)
- Together we will map out and navigate your journey to reach your goal and achieve the results you desire
- You no longer have to work/travel alone

Ha is a member of:
Certified Coaches Federation, Rescue Institute, Straight Forward Coaching

Navigate Your Way to Success
Companion Workbook
By
Ha Tran

Please visit: www.hope-empowered.com

About The Author

Ha Tran is a successful businesswoman, a Navigational Coach certified as a Master Mind executive coach, life and business coach, and inspirational speaker. She came to the United States from Vietnam as a war refugee in 1979 with her husband and two young sons. She and her family settled in Illinois where their two daughters were born.

Ha obtained her Associate's Degree in Science at Illinois Valley Community College, and her Bachelor's Degree in Science in Economics at Illinois State University, Normal, Illinois.

In 1989 Ha and her family moved to Massachusetts, where she used her considerable skills in management working for an insurance company and two technology firms. In 2004 she started her own business, Ultimate Office Solutions, working with companies to improve their overall performance and revenue.

As a Navigational Coach, Ha now works with individuals and companies.

Ha is an inspirational speaker and has founded Hope-Empowered to spread her message. Her mission is to motivate, inspire, inform, enlighten, encourage, support, and empower people to conquer their obstacles and to live with a promise in their heart...*hope*.

Ha currently lives on the North Shore of Massachusetts with her husband. She speaks, teaches, and lectures around the country. Visit her website at www.hope-empowered.com